Further volumes in the series
General Editor: MIRIAM KOCHAN

Gertrude Bell   SUSAN GOODMAN
Mme de Staël   RENEE WINEGARTEN
Emily Dickinson   DONNA DICKENSON
Elizabeth Gaskell   TESSA BRODETSKY

In preparation
Anna Freud   RENEE PATON
Marie Stopes   SUSAN GOODMAN
George Sand   DONNA DICKENSON
Clara Schumann   GLENDA ABRAMSON
Simone Weil   PAT LITTLE
Emily Carr   RUTH GOWERS

C'est ainsi que la Verité
Pour mïeux établir sa puissance,
A pris les traits de la bauté,
Et les graces de l'Eloquence.

Mme du Châtelet

Esther Ehrman

BERG *Leamington Spa*

Published in 1986 by **Berg Publishers Ltd**
24 Binswood Avenue, Leamington Spa, CV32 5SQ, UK

British Library Cataloguing in Publication Data

Ehrman, Esther
    Mme du Chatelet.—(Berg women's series)
    1. Châtelet, Emile. marquise du   2. France—
    Biography
    I. Title
    944'.034'0924   DC135.C4/
    ISBN 0–907582–90–7   1000742942
    ISBN 0–907582–85–0 Pbk

Library of Congress Cataloging-in-Publication Data

Ehrman, Esther.
    Mme. du Châtelet.

    (Berg women's series)
    Bibliography: p.
    Includes index.
    1. Du Châtelet, Gabrielle Emilie Le Tonnelier de
Breteuil, marquise, 1706–1749. 2. Authors, French—
18th century—Biography. 3. Scientists—France—
Biography. I. Title. II. Series.
PQ1981.D55Z64 1986   848'.509 [B]   86–4231
ISBN 0–907582–90–7
ISBN 0–907582–85–0 (pbk.)

Printed in Great Britain by Oxford University Press, Oxford

Contents

Illustrations

The portrait of Mme du Châtelet on the cover is from an
engraving, Bibliothèque Nationale ref. N2, and is reproduced by
permission of the Bibliothèque Nationale, Paris

Introduction

Mme Newton-Pompom du Châtelet, the name Voltaire affectionately gives to his friend, is telling even if it does not tell all. She does, indeed, have a love for pompoms, for ornaments and luxuries of every sort. She has an equal passion for science. Her uniqueness probably stems from her determination — and she is a very determined person — to make such a combination acceptable: all the female pleasures and privileges as well as intellectual equality with men. The twentieth century has hardly achieved universal recognition for such a dual image. The eighteenth century just laughed at it. The intellectual woman was by no means unknown. The image of the *femme savante*, the bluestocking mocked by Molière for her exclusive love of learning was no fantasy. In that image there was no room for such 'common' things as feelings or ordinary human relationships. That is not Mme du Châtelet's ideal. She wants equal opportunities for women and pleads for their proper education.

'If I were king,' she writes, 'I would redress an abuse which cuts back, as it were, one half of human kind. I would have women participate in all human rights, especially those of the mind.' She complains, 'There is no place where we are trained to think' and suggests that that is why 'at no time in the course of so many centuries, a good tragedy, a good poem, a respected tale, a fine painting, a good book on physics has ever been produced by a woman'.

She herself had been trained to think, a rare privilege which her father had been wealthy enough and perceptive enough to offer her and which she strenuously pursued until the end of her life. It is a rather interesting feature of the period that one could, as Mme du Châtelet did, engage the most distinguished scientists of the day for tutorials in advanced mathematics.

Mme du Châtelet's intellectual skills, a good working knowledge of English, Latin, Italian and mathematics, made her an ideal partner for the Anglophile Voltaire with his admiration for Newton, Locke and Pope; she read their work in the original, of course. It also made her one of a new breed, as it were, of

1

Europeans, the French section of which was to be found among the *philosophes*, keen to compare ideas, values, lifestyles and to extrapolate universal truths and truths about the universe on the basis of such comparisons, truths which could replace the 'outdated' teachings of religion and political theory. The intelligent French reader in the *philosophe* camp was ready for the European and Mme du Châtelet was one of the few able and willing to act as interpreter.

The main attraction was England and Mme du Châtelet translated two works, one on morals and one on science. The moral work was Bernard Mandeville's entertaining *The Fable of the Bees*, which turned accepted notions on their head with its thesis that private vice is public benefit — prostitution keeps husbands happy and their families stable, filthy streets are an indication of a bustling, prosperous society. The scientific work was Newton's *Principia Mathematica*. Mme du Châtelet's mansion, the famous Cirey, became the setting for the Newtonian camp waging battle against the old Cartesian order. A laboratory was set up, scientists were invited from Paris and from abroad and everyone 'Newtonised'.

With the fashion for English thought went an empirical approach to all questions, an urge for scientific proof and demonstration. Mme du Châtelet appreciated this but she does not accept it as the only method. She is convinced that where scientific demonstration ends reason may take over the demonstrating. There are, as she puts it, 'a number of points in metaphysics which lend themselves to demonstrations just as rigorous as the demonstrations of geometry, even if they are different in kind'; she would like to find a form of calculation in metaphysics comparable to calculation in geometry. Metaphysics was a German speciality and so she turned to Germany and to the metaphysics of Leibniz and set before her French readers in her book *Institutions de physique*, the necessary truth of the existence of God, the structure of matter in terms of monads and the argument that this is the best of all possible worlds.

While God, as first cause, provided a useful back-up for the scientists' universe, no *philosophe* would accept divine prescription for moral conduct, since that would mean accepting the validity of revealed doctrines and of documents such as the Bible. Intellectual self-respect, however, demanded reasoned demonstration, showing why it was to be rejected, so Mme du Châtelet and Voltaire duly studied the Bible and Mme du Châtelet's thoughts are set out in her *Examen de la Genèse*. Her new role as critic is not as significant as her contribution expounding or translating the ideas of others. Inevitably, she looks for logic where it does not apply and reads motives into the text which she then indignantly rejects. For instance, to make death the punishment for not obeying the law of circumcision is, she writes, 'just like damning all children who die without baptism', echoing here the worry of a number of *philosophes*. The biblical text does not speak of death but of being 'cut off from his people'. Her commentary was never published.

Mme du Châtelet is much more comfortable exploring the 'natural' logic of grammar in her *Grammaire raisonnée*, of which only three chapters are extant. Since the mind operates in the same way in all places on earth, natural rules can be determined. Grammar, in her view, describes how language represents mental processes — 'operations of the soul on the objects of our ideas' is her formulation. The three chapters are often ingenious; her recognition of the role usage has shows that she is not unduly rigid in her approach.

Lastly, a very personal work published in the eighteenth century and again recently, her *Discours sur le bonheur*. Here, for a moment, it might appear that a *femme savante* is writing. A love of study is essential, she tells us, especially for women, whom it can compensate for all they have to endure; a talent for illusion is needed, too. It is a wistful essay with gentle nostalgia for happiness only recently lost.

Mme du Châtelet's writings earn her a reputation as a scholar, a *savante*. She never flaunts her scholarship. The ladies playing cards with her at the Queen's table had no idea, Voltaire tells us, that they were sitting next to Newton's commentator. Nor probably did those who watched her acting and singing in the frequent performances given in her own house, Cirey, or in those of her friends. Her writings are serious, her personality is not. They are learned, she is shocking. Whether determined to storm the men's citadel of the café dressed as a man, or striding through street crowds 'dripping with diamonds' or jumping into a carriage immediately behind the queen, to the speechless horror of ladies who believed that that place was rightfully theirs, she usually had someone worried.

A number of biographies have been written about Mme du Châtelet. All have focused on her life with Voltaire. While the sixteen years she spent with him are undoubtedly important in the documentation of his life, the light which such documentation shed on her shows her to have been a fascinating representative of a society in which she lived fully, *femme* and *savante*.

1 The World of Mme du Châtelet

Mme du Châtelet belonged to what was, in many ways, an elite society. She was at home with kings and queens and with the highest nobles in the land. As a member of that aristocracy, she was part of a world with a never-ending social round in royal courts, salons and cafés. She was also accepted by the best intellectuals of the day and, as *philosophe*, belonged to an intellectual elite keenly interested in the cultural and political life of Europe. Her society enjoyed some of the finest painting and music that France has known. Contemporary artists included Watteau, whose paintings representing theatrical performers against a backdrop of painted scenery and dramatic landscape were frequently copied. His scenes adorned Mme du Châtelet's bathroom while one of her portraits was the work of the fashionable painter of pastel portraits, Maurice Quentin de la Tour. Musically talented, Mme du Châtelet gave recitals of works by Rameau who dominated the musical scene at the time and was made Master of the King's Music in 1745. In this society, however, she was but one person among many. For months at a time, she lived away from this world as the lady of a provincial manor, Cirey, where she was thrown back onto her own resources of study and home entertainment. It was as the mistress of Cirey that Mme du Châtelet became famous.

Cirey, Home and Centre of Learning

The manor was a large house with extensive grounds at Cirey, a property inherited by her husband, the Marquis du Châtelet. It was situated in a corner of Champagne and, although isolated, was not beyond the reach of visitors from Paris or, more easily, from Lorraine and the court of Stanislas, ex-King of Poland, at Lunéville. Various accounts exist of visits to Cirey, accounts which tend to vary with the mood of the writer or the reception given them.

An early visitor, M. de Villefort,[1] tells of a house shuttered and in darkness when it was broad daylight outside, of being led through deserted rooms by a servant with a lantern, to arrive at a drawing-room brilliantly lit by twenty candles; there he stood facing the lady of the house who was seated at a writing table, adorned with glittering diamonds, surrounded by sheets of paper and scientific instruments, and he was thence led up a secret staircase to the room of Voltaire. Then came a bell, which summoned them to the dining-room — it had two hatches, one for food, one for dirty dishes, but no servants. After supper, another bell for readings on philosophy, another at bedtime and yet another at 4 am for poetry readings. A later account by Mme de Graffigny, in 1738, shows Voltaire's wing, exquisite, with gilded panelling and chinoiserie furniture and little statues on lacquer bases in a gallery over thirty feet long which led from his rooms. Even better were the rooms of the marquise, also panelled, in yellow and blue, where everything was matching, even the dog's basket (possibly the original for the blue and yellow colours of Queen Astarte in Voltaire's *Zadig*), then a tiny boudoir, each panel of which had a picture by Watteau and, most sensational of all, a bathroom lined with tiles, a marble floor and porcelain baths. An attendant *cabinet de toilette* had green carved and gilded panels, a sofa and chairs, also carved and gilded and a painted ceiling: All of this is contrasted to the guest's room, large and dingy, with one draughty, ill-fitting window, old-fashioned chairs, a chest of drawers and one table by the bed. No one saw the lady of the house between midday and supper time at 9 pm; the long hours were devoted to study.

However, time, at Cirey, was not entirely devoted to study. A small theatre was set up, actors were brought and hosts, relations, guests and neighbours performed; there were times, writes Mme de Graffigny, when the days were spent learning parts and rehearsing and whole nights were given to acting and singing — after one midnight supper Mme du Châtelet was to sing a whole opera.

In the summer of 1734, when Voltaire first escaped there to avoid the police and the *lettre de cachet* after the public burning of his *Lettres philosophiques*, Cirey had none of these facilities. It had been standing empty for years and Voltaire enjoyed making building plans for the house and the grounds. Architecture was a fashionable aristocratic pastime that even royalty indulged in; both

The Château de Cirey

Louis XV and Stanislas loved planning new buildings. When Mme du Châtelet arrived in Cirey a few months after Voltaire, she, too, threw herself into the renovating. Not that she always had the same ideas as Voltaire. She had doors put where he had planned windows, a staircase where he had wanted a chimney piece.[2] But he was happy to bow to her wishes and laid out much of the money needed to put their plans into effect.

They ordered and brought books and instruments in large quantities to Cirey. They studied Newton and set up experiments; they read and discussed philosophy, they had daily Bible sessions of text analysis; they acted and entertained their friends and such guests as would make the journey to Cirey. Most of these shared their interests and belonged to that specifically eighteenth-century category of intellectuals known as *les philosophes*.

Les Philosophes

'Every century which thinks,' wrote d'Alembert in his *Essai des Elemens de philosophie*,[3] 'be it well or badly, and which thinks otherwise than the century which preceded it prides itself on the title *philosophe* . . . our century has thus called itself the century of philosophy par excellence'. This 'thinking otherwise', this 'basic opposition to the fundamental conceptions underlying the dominant current of thought of the previous age, and indeed of earlier times', as Niklaus writes,[4] constitutes, in his opinion, the main contribution of French eighteenth-century thought to the history of ideas. The instrument with which this opposition was fashioned — namely reason — had acquired renewed status since the work of Descartes in the seventeenth century. It was not, however, until the end of the authoritarian rule of Louis XIV, that writers became bold enough to apply this instrument to every sphere of authority, to re-examine, in the light of reason, the human condition and the universe, the physical and metaphysical world, and to challenge established and received ideas in all these spheres. This inevitably created an opposition between the establishment in matters of religion, government, literature and science on the one hand and the challengers, the *philosophes*, on the other.

The voices of the *philosophes* were at first few and isolated. Censorship, public burning of 'subversive' works, exile (at least from Paris), *lettres de cachet* and imprisonment proved effective deterrents for many and it took nearly half a century before there was what could be seen as a movement of *philosophes*, with a rallying point, the *Encyclopédie* of Diderot and d'Alembert.

Battle lines were by no means always clear-cut; nor were all confrontations necessarily aggressive. The *philosophes* numbered among them many of the greatest writers of the day — Montesquieu, Voltaire, Diderot, to name but the best known — and their work was appreciated by the cultured reader throughout France as well as abroad. Part of their dangerousness lay in their skill. Where before a very limited readership would be able to discuss the basis of religious belief and morality, scientific theories or legal and political reforms, the *philosophes*' brief was to ensure that such matters became accessible to reason, a tool available to all, and thus carried with it the involvement of the whole literate world, which included the establishments. There was thus a certain pride in the *philosophes*' achievement and an exposure to their ideas, persuasively presented.

The most virulent confrontation, as might be expected, was the one with the religious establishment. The *philosophes* were happy to adopt the ideas of the English deists. Reason welcomed the idea of a necessary Being, the first cause in the creation of the universe, the regulator of its laws and the source of meaning for its every aspect and part. But reason was, by definition, incapable of accepting truths and values based on revelation. Mme du Châtelet's commentary on the Bible, *Examen de la Genèse*, is typical in that she sets out to demonstrate the irrationality of statements as, for instance, who would Cain have been afraid of, since there were hardly any other human beings yet, or of sequences, as, for example, how could there have been an evening and a morning at the end of the first day of creation since the sun and moon were only to be created on the fourth day. This kind of picking holes into detail was the method which would 'prove' the absurdity of the whole, a method the reader of Voltaire's *Candide* will easily recognise.

Ethics and the moral code, traditionally linked with revealed religions, could clearly not be jettisoned by the *philosophes*; so here, too, reason looked for alternative norms. To the question 'what is virtue?', one answer was 'it is the faithful fulfilment of obligations dictated to us by reason'.[5] Reason could also see and analyse the ills of society and, on the basis of such analyses, prescribe the most suitable remedies. All this led to an optimistic outlook, a confidence that man had it in his power to improve his lot. Before this could be achieved, however, the wrongs of society, the hypocrisy and corruption had to be constantly denounced. This, too, the *philosophes* took upon themselves. This may have been the attraction for Mme du Châtelet of Mandeville's *The Fable of the Bees*, 'the best moral book ever written' in her view and one which she set out to translate.

In such a climate of thought, it was clear that science and philosophy would make great strides. Reason was not only an instrument of logical analysis but the interpreter of scientific evidence. Here, too, Mme du Châtelet participated, as one of the first to make the work of Newton accessible in France.

There was, indeed, no field of civilisation barred to the *philosophe*. As d'Alembert wrote: 'From the principles of the profane sciences to the foundations of revelation, from metaphysics to matters of taste, from music to morals, from the scholastic disputes of theologians to objects of commerce, from the rights of princes to that of peoples, from natural law to the arbitrary law of nations . . . everything has been debated, analysed . . . aired.'[6]

It should perhaps be stressed that the revolutionary activity of the Enlightenment, of the *philosophes* enlightened by reason, was purely intellectual and advisory. There was no question, yet, of militant action. The *philosophes* noted with sadness but without any sense of despair the fact that when one of the most distinguished members in their ranks, the royal Prince Frederick of Prussia, who, in his correspondence with Voltaire and with Mme du Châtelet, shared and encouraged their interests and their enthusiasms, became king, he put none of it into practice.

One further feature of the *philosophes*, evident in the life and work of Mme du Châtelet, is a certain elitism. All men may be endowed with reason, but not all have the ability to make the best use of it. 'Thinking people', 'civilised men of the world', these are the readers Mme du Châtelet addresses specifically, a category of person she expects to find among the socially and financially well endowed.[7]

Society, its Cafés and Salons, its Card Games

Entry into the social world of courts and salons was largely reserved to members of the aristocracy and of the world of letters. Mme du Châtelet belonged to both. It was a life that demanded great energy, of which Mme du Châtelet fortunately had an abundance. She would go to the park with Mme de Saint-Pierre, to the theatre with Mme d'Aiguillon, to the Jardin du Roi with Fontenelle; she supped with Mme Rohan, with Mme de Luxembourg, with Mme de Brancas — and still found time to read all the latest books. She travelled everywhere, to St-Maur, to Chantilly, to Creteil, a hundred leagues and back to see her mother on a five-day journey, without sleep; on to Versailles, to Fontainebleau; in town to l'Hôtel de Richelieu, to the Chevalier d'Hautefort, to the Venetian ambassadress — and on.[8]

The world of courts, salons and cafés was the all-important arbiter of fashions and taste, especially in Paris: it provided the stimulus for the best minds of the day. This privileged section of society supplied the readership for the *philosophes* and the critics of the theatre. Consequently, much of what was written in the eighteenth century was pitched to their level of interest. A writer would need to flatter their intelligence and understanding to get a hearing, so much so that such flattery was to be seen as an abuse and to be denounced in the second half of the century by such writers as, for example, Jean-Jacques Rousseau, in his *Discours sur les sciences et les arts* and Diderot, in his *Neveu de Rameau*, as demeaning the writer's message. At the same time, it was a readership with intellectual curiosity, happy to be informed about scholarly and scientific work and have it made accessible in a popularised form. Hence the fashions for the latest theories in astronomy and physics, the furious debates for and against Descartes, Newton and Leibniz. This was the market for Mme du Châtelet's *Institutions de physique*, with its much praised clear account of the ideas of the German philosophers, and for her translation of Newton's *Principia Mathematica*. It was also a milieu which appreciated intrigue and gossip, preferably in rhyme.

Much of this originated in the cafés of Paris, meeting places which were mainly for men, though Mme du Châtelet and a very few other women were also to be seen there. Coffee drinking was a fashionable ritual which Montesquieu had already mocked in

1721, in his *Lettres persanes*. Cafés were of fairly recent origin since coffee was a new drink introduced to the nobles of the court of Louis XIV by the Turkish ambassador. Doctors, horrified, had spread the rumour that it was a deadly poison, which made it the more daring and smart a thing to drink.

By 1720, Paris had apparently become one great café area. Every apothecary sold coffee and served it at his counter. For a time it replaced cabarets and alcohol and was therefore hailed as ennobling manners and conducive to temperance, virtue and the rule of the intellect. Hamel[9] tells how François Procope, of the famous café bearing his name, first peddled his liquor in the open air, then had a coffee stall, then a shop and finally salons elegantly decorated with mirrors and gilt mouldings, where famous people shared a spacious divan and took refreshments. 'Fine ladies stopped their carriages at the door and waited there until they had finished drinking their cup of coffee, served on a silver saucer'.

Most famous were the Café Procope, the Café Gradot, the Café Laurent and the Café de la Régence — the latter specialising in games of chess and draughts. At the Café Buci, the *Gazette* and the *Mercure de France* could be read and tobacco was offered free with the coffee. Many had their special clientele; theatre critics, actors and dancers were to be seen at the Café Procope; here Fontenelle, Diderot and their friends would talk literature, politics, philosophy and religion, inventing a special vocabulary: religion was 'javotte', the soul was 'Margot', God was 'M. de l'Être'. They would criticise new plays and Voltaire's secretary, Longchamp, tells how Voltaire dressed up as a priest, with a cassock and long cloak, black stockings, girdle and bands and an unpowdered wig, a breviary in his hand, to hear what was being said about his latest play, *Sémiramis* after the second night — he apparently did not enjoy the experience.[10]

At the Café Laurent a couplet war was waged; it was the meeting place for poets, musicians and painters. At the Café Gradot were the scientists, astronomers, geometers and serious writers; among them was Maupertuis and, knowing that she could find him there, Mme du Châtelet.

As distinct from the cafés, the famous literary salons of the period were ruled over by women. There were some forty salons and Mme du Châtelet was to be seen in several. Already as a child of ten, her parents' salon had accustomed her to salon ways. Some twenty people would gather every evening at l'Hôtel de Breteuil; Fontenelle would come on Thursdays; other guests included the Duc de Saint-Simon, the poet Jean-Baptiste and the young man who was to become her greatest friend, Voltaire.

In the 1730s, one of her favourite salons was l'Hôtel de Brancas which, according to Grimm,[11] was in its time what l'Hôtel de Rambouillet had been a century earlier, a place where mental tournaments were fought before a society which always applauded the strongest. It was, he wrote, an institute of wit rather than a temple dedicated to friendship; there, one might spend years on terms of intimate friendship with one another, yet without ever liking or esteeming one's fellows. The account Grimm gives was written several decades on; Mme du Châtelet certainly found the atmosphere congenial — she kept the friends she made there.

Not all such hôtels were in Paris. Mme du Châtelet and Voltaire were well received at Sceaux by the Duchesse du Maine, when they escaped there after Voltaire's famous gaffe at Versailles: Mme du Châtelet, guest of the queen, had lost an inordinate amount of money, some 80,000 *livres*, at cards and Voltaire, exasperated, was heard to say, in English: 'Did you not know, that you was playing with cheats?' Not surprisingly, his words were understood and the couple departed abruptly, to Sceaux, to the Duchesse du Maine, grand-daughter of the great Condé and renowned hostess for nearly half a century. There is an amusing account of their arrival in a letter from Mme de Staal to Mme du Deffand, neither of whom was particularly fond of Mme du Châtelet: 'Mme du Châtelet and Voltaire made their appearance yesternight, near midnight, like two spectres, with an odour of embalming about them, as if just out of their tombs. We were rising from the table; the spectres, however, were hungry; they needed supper and, what is more, beds, which were not ready.'[12] On this particular occasion they stayed barely a fortnight and kept well hidden: 'Our ghosts do not show themselves in daylight', though their presence was very much felt. Mme du Châtelet moved rooms three times, not finding things to her liking and appropriated all the tables she could find. On another visit they participated fully in the life at Sceaux, acting Voltaire's plays and not hesitating to invite numerous guests of their own to the performances. The acting was apparently good: 'Miss Piggery [Mme du Châtelet] put over the extravagance of her role so perfectly that it gave me very real pleasure', comments Mme de Staal.

Hospitality was apparently unbounded and nowhere more so than at Lunéville, the court of the queen's father, Stanislas Leczszinski, ex-King of Poland, Duc de Lorraine et de Bar. Invited by Stanislas, Mme du Châtelet and Voltaire stayed there for a first visit early in 1748. 'Life is one long entertainment', writes Mme du Châtelet. 'I do nothing but perform opera and comedy.'[13] But it was here that, only one year later, the king was to prepare and furnish a special lodging for Mme du Châtelet's confinement, where she duly gave birth and six days later, died.

The court of Lunéville in Lorraine at the crossroads — as Mme du Châtelet claimed — to Versailles and to Switzerland, attracted many distinguished guests and, guided by Stanislas and his talented mistress, Mme de Boufflers, assembled a European community of intellectuals and aristocrats. Stanislas himself was a conciliatory figure, seemingly unaware of the countless intrigues around him. He paid every respect to religious observance, directed by his confessor, le Père Menoux, a Jesuit, while also tolerating the views of such as Mme du Châtelet and Voltaire. He genuinely welcomed them and yet funded the publications of one of Voltaire's greatest enemies, l'Abbé Desfontaines. It is not clear whether Voltaire was aware of this. Stanislas clearly tried to satisfy everyone. The poor king, wrote Voltaire, had trouble every day after mass, patching up matters with his mistress and with his confessor, le Père Menoux. The latter had hoped that Stanislas might replace Mme de Boufflers, perhaps with Mme du Châtelet, and journeyed to Cirey in person to deliver the king's invitation. Unfortunately, the two women shared the same views and the same enthusiasm for the pleasures of life. Mme de Boufflers, a wit at all times, wrote her own epitaph:

> Profoundly peaceful, here she lies,
> The Lady Volupté below
> Who, to make sure of Paradise
> Enjoyed it ere she had to go.

The guests included Mme de Graffigny, who had also visited Cirey and to whom we owe the lively account of life there. She was happy at Lunéville, writing popular novels and plays. Central, too, among the guests was her friend 'Pan-Pan', François-Étienne Devaux, poet of madrigals and verse for special occasions. The favourite, as far as the ladies were concerned, and father of Mme du Châtelet's child, was the handsome Jean-François Saint-Lambert, who much preferred literature and salon life to his army career. There was also a dwarf.[14]

Conversation, acting, cards, all could be indulged at Lunéville. It is perhaps more surprising that it was possible for guests to opt out of the court life. Mme du Châtelet, in the last months of her pregnancy, was working feverishly to finish her commentary on Newton's *Principia Mathematica*, which she had already translated. In a letter to Saint-Lambert, she writes an account of her days: 'I get up at nine o'clock, sometimes at eight; I work until three and take up my work again at four; I stop at ten to eat a bite. Until midnight I chat with M. de Voltaire who is present at my supper, then I take up my work again at midnight until five o'clock.'[15]

There was one society pastime which took up a great deal of Mme du Châtelet's time — and money: playing cards. In eighteenth-century France, as in England, card games were a widespread passion, 'an enchanting witchery, gotten between Idleness and Avarice' as the first page of the *Compleat Gamester* describes it in 1725. In France, Louis XV and the queen seem to have been addicts. The king would not miss his game even when he was ill; the queen was known to be gambling for at least one hour every day.[16] While such games were by no means new, the greatest number of card games came into being in the eighteenth century in France.[17] In every social sphere, beginning with royalty, a great deal of money changed hands at these games and we know that Mme du Châtelet lost vast sums in this, probably her only serious indulgence. At the court of Versailles she played at the queen's table, the game played there being most frequently *cavagnole*; at Lunéville, court of Stanislas of Poland, the fashionable game was *comète*. *Cavagnole* seems to have been something like bingo, players each setting out a pack of cards on the table and drawing numbers out of a bag when it was their turn. Since this was the queen's favourite game, Voltaire's little rhyme was not exactly appreciated:

FRANÇOIS, MARIE,

ARQUET, DE VOLTAIRE.

Né à Paris le 21. Novembre 1694.

Voltaire, a contemporary engraving

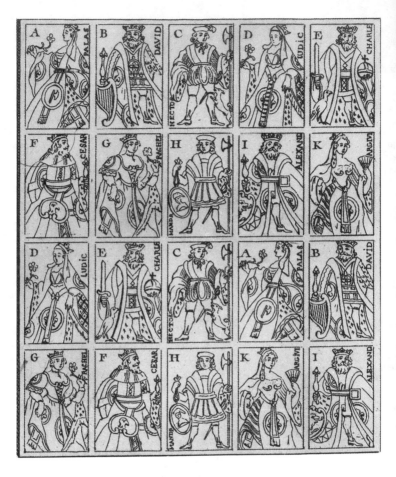

Eighteenth-century playing cards,
from *l'Encyclopédie*, Paris, 1763

> You may think gambling can console
> But boredom nears with steady steps
> The table of the *cavagnole*
> And sits between two crowned heads.

Comète apparently required two packs and had two special *comète* cards used as jokers; the name, it was suggested, derived from the long series of cards thrown down by a player, like a trail of light behind a comet.

The printing of cards was a serious craft, each region had the right to print its own variety and some were most beautiful. As all things had to have a meaning, various theories set out to explain the different suits and figures: hearts stood for the Church, spades were warriors, clubs were the labourers and diamonds, *carreaux*, were tile-shaped and stood for the bourgeois whose house was often tiled. The four kings in the pack bore the names David, Alexander, Caesar and Charlemagne, indicating the Jewish, Greek, Roman and German monarchies; while the four queens, Rachel, Judith, Pallas and Argine — an anagram of Regina — symbolised four kinds of rule, through beauty, piety, wisdom and right of birth.

Gaming houses sprang up everywhere although they were forbidden for some time. A high tax on cards aroused much discussion; Diderot's *Encyclopédie* wholeheartedly approved. In 1751, the *Encyclopédie* devoted an extensive article to the subject and, as might be expected from the *philosophe* camp, gave moral advice to the monarch:

> As a ruler must be concerned to prevent the ruin of citizens in all dealings of this kind, it behoves him to regulate this one and to see how far the interest of the state and of individual persons makes it necessary for him either to prohibit gaming or to allow it to all. The laws of wise governments can never be too harsh on the Academies of Philocubus.[18]

Characteristic, too, of the *philosophes* is the psychological analysis: 'It holds the soul in a kind of agitation, movement, ecstasy and this without requiring serious attention, something our lazy nature is delighted to dispense with.'[19]

Mme du Châtelet agreed, to some extent; the satisfaction of

gaming lies 'in the excitement of the soul', she wrote. But for her, this heightened the quality of life by heightening the awareness of every sense and fibre of being.[20] She agreed that dangers were involved, but she saw gaming as a passion that linked humanity together, one which the *philosophe* could understand in others of inferior station because he could identify with the experience.[21]

Notes

1. For an English account of this visit, in 1736, cf. S. Edwards, *The Divine Mistress*.
2. Voltaire correspondence, October 1734.
3. Cf. R. Niklaus, 'The Age of Enlightenment', in *The Age of Enlightenment*, p. 395.
4. Ibid., p. 407.
5. Toussaint, *Des Moeurs*, Paris 1748.
6. d'Alembert, *Essai des Elémens de philosophie*, quoted in Niklaus, 'The Age of Enlightenment', pp. 395–7.
7. *Discours sur le bonheur*.
8. F. Hamel, *An Eighteenth-Century Marquise*, ch. 4, p. 130.
9. Ibid., p. 186.
10. Longchamp, *Voltaire et Mme du Châtelet*.
11. *Correspondance Littéraire*, May 1771.
12. A. Maurel, *La Marquise du Châtelet, amie de Voltaire*, Appendix: Letter dated Tuesday 15 August 1747.
13. Letter dated 30 November 1748.
14. Cf. G. Doscot, *Stanislas Leszczynski et la cour de Lorraine*, pp. 173ff.
15. Letter of June 1749.
16. J. Dunkley, *Gambling, A Social and Moral Problem in France, 1685–1792*, p. 22.
17. Cf. H. R. d'Allemagne, *Les Cartes à jouer du 14ème au 20ème siécle*, pp. 455ff.
18. *Encyclopédie ou Dictionnaire raisonné des sciences, des arts et des métiers*, Paris 1751, vol. 2, article *Jeux*.
19. Ibid., p. 59.
20. *Discours sur le Bonheur*.
21. Translation of *The Fable of the Bees*.

2 Life of an Eighteenth-Century Marquise

Gabrielle Émilie Le Tonnelier de Breteuil, Marquise du Châtelet-Laumont, was born on 17 December, 1706, a fact only established nearly a hundred years after her death.[1] She died in 1749. As the long aristocratic name indicates, the family was well connected. Her father, Louis-Nicolas, Baron de Breteuil, owned land in Touraine and a well-situated house in Paris. A favourite of Louis XIV, he had been a great charmer in his youth, with a number of 'scandals' to his name. One lady, a cousin, Marie Le Fèvre de Caumartin, had to take refuge in a convent when she found she was pregnant, and became his wife three days before she died. Another, Anne Bellinzani, a lively and intelligent lady with a keen interest in Italian poetry and scientific discoveries, had fallen in love with Louis-Nicolas at the age of fourteen and later bore him a daughter, Michelle. Michelle was put into a convent, discovered the identity of her mother many years later and, at the age of fifty, started proceedings against her. Gabrielle Émilie was to help this half-sister of hers. Not much seems to be known of Gabrielle Émilie's mother, Gabrielle Anne de Froulay. Louis-Nicolas married her when he was forty-five, in 1697, at which point he settled down, and was allowed to buy the position of Master of Protocol for Ambassadors at Court, a position for which he payed 120,000 *livres*, more than twice the sum he would allow for the dowry of his daughter. When Louis XIV died in 1715, Louis-Nicolas retired from the court; Gabrielle Émilie was nine years old. They lived in the large Paris house overlooking the Tuileries, a house with four floors, each of which, with its eight or nine rooms, was allocated to different members of the family. Louis-Nicolas and his wife had the first floor, of which three rooms were for books; on the second floor lived his sister-in-law, the dowager Comtesse de Breteuil-Charmeaux; on the third, two men, le Commandeur de Breteuil-Chanteclerc and Augustin de Breteuil-Conti, Bishop of Rennes. The fourth floor was for the five children. Later, in her correspondence, Gabrielle Émilie, the

17

second youngest, only speaks of her half-sister and of her younger brother, l'Abbé de Breteuil. She herself stood out as a somewhat ungainly teenager. 'My Cousin Émilie', writes Mme de Créqui,[2] 'was three or four years younger than I, but five or six inches taller. . . . She was a colossus in all her limbs — a marvel of strength and a prodigy of clumsiness. She had terrible feet and formidable hands.'

Émilie was a great learner and was tutored in Latin, Italian — by her father — English, mathematics and the sciences, acquiring a much more serious education than most young ladies were likely to receive in her day. Like her mother, writes Vaillot, Émilie was studious and disciplined; like her father, rash and spontaneous. At her parents' evenings in l'Hôtel Breteuil she probably listened with interest to the conversation of the distinguished guests, many of them regular visitors, such as Fontenelle and Voltaire with whom she was to renew her acquaintance within a few years.

At the age of nineteen, on 20 June, 1725, with a dowry of only 50,000 *livres*, Gabrielle Émilie was married to Florent Claude Chastellet, eldest son of Florent, Marquis du Chastellet (the spelling Châtelet was introduced by Voltaire). She married into a family proud of its military achievements, which could trace its ancestors back to the sons of Charlemagne and to crusaders with Godefroy de Bouillon. The marquis inherited the estate of Cirey in Champagne from his mother and, shortly after the wedding, was given the government of Semur-en-Auxois in Burgundy by his father. After a brief season in Paris, the couple set off for Semur at the end of September 1725. A graphic accounts tells of their reception by the town of Semur whose inhabitants turned out in strength to welcome them. Church bells rang out, the mayor read an address. Led by mounted guards, the new governor's carriages and his retinue passed under an 'arc de triomphe' erected in honour of the marquise; they were followed by courtiers with gold-tipped canes, by gentry on horse and on foot complete with their swords, by the notables of the bourgeoisie in tight culottes and by archers closing the cortège, which was flanked by soldiers of the militia. The marquise was dressed 'à la polonaise', the latest Paris fashion; her husband wore his uniform of Colonel of the Regiment of Hainaut. They were received at the castle with sweet preserves, and the town's welcome culminated in a grand ball with a finale of fireworks.[3]

For the next few years, until 1732, the marquise was a frequent visitor to Semur. She made improvements to the house and redesigned the gardens. Her second child, a son, Florent-Louis Marie du Chastellet, was born at Semur in November, 1727; her first child, a daughter, was born in the summer of 1726, in the house of Marie-Catherine Armande de Richelieu, a relation by marriage and sister of the Duc de Richelieu, a brilliant young man, who later became one of the marquise's intimate friends. The Marquis du Chastellet was mostly absent on garrison duty. The marquise lived in his town house in Paris, rue de Saint-Honoré. When her father died, in 1728, her mother retired to a country house at Créteil. Her daughter periodically paid courtesy visits.

Left to her own devices, the marquise threw herself into the social whirl of salons, opera, theatre and gambling frequently in the company of her best friend, the Duchesse de Saint-Pierre — niece of the famous minister of Louis XIV, Colbert — and of one or other of the two sons of Louis de Brancas, to whose free-thinking salon the marquise was a regular visitor.

The marquise's first documented 'affair' was with the Comte de Guébriant, a womaniser, some seven or eight years older than herself. The marquise was much more serious about it than he would have liked and he tried to disentangle himself. An oft-told anecdote recounts how the marquise begged him to visit her one last time and how, when he wished to leave, she asked him to pass her the bowl of soup from the mantelpiece; he did so and she handed him a note, not to be opened until he was in the street. Once there, he read: 'I die poisoned by your hand'. He rushed back. What action he took, says Vaillot, is not clear, but no harm ensued. Another version has it that she wrote a farewell letter to the comte, telling him that she wished to die since she was no longer the sole object of his life. When he rushed over to her house in case she did anything rash, he was refused entry, but forced his way in and found her apparently asleep having taken enough opium to kill herself. 'He sent for help, saved her life, but as he felt unable to attach himself to her in spite of this proof of her love, she consoled herself with several other men.'[4] It was clearly much talked-about. The 'other men' were to be people whose intellectual stature mattered much more to her, the Duc de

19

Richelieu, Maupertuis and Voltaire.

A famous pen-portrait of the marquise by one of the great *salonnières* of the period, Mme du Deffand, describes her appearance and character. The vicious description, a number of versions of which were in circulation, would seem to indicate that Mme du Châtelet was seen as a potentially dangerous rival by Mme du Deffand.

Imagine a tall, dry female with a flushed complexion, a sharp face, a pointed nose and you have the face of the fair Émilie, a face with which she is so satisfied that she spares no effort to show it off, hairstyle, pompoms, stone and glass jewellery, everything in great profusion; but as she wants to be beautiful in spite of nature and magnificent in spite of fortune, she is obliged to have her luxuries by doing without necessities, for instance chemises and other like trifles.

She was born with a fair intellect; a desire to make this appear even better made her prefer the study of the most abstract sciences to knowledge of a more pleasing kind. She thinks that in this singular way she will attain a greater reputation and a decided superiority over all other women.

She has not limited her ambition to this but wished to be a princess and she has succeeded, not by the grace of God nor of the king, but on her own. She has since dropped this ridiculous trait like many another and people have come to see in her a stage princess, almost forgetting that she is a lady of rank. The lady works so hard to appear what she is not that one no longer knows what she really is. Even her faults may well not be natural to her, but be linked to her pretensions; her lack of regard to that of status of princess, her dry manner to that of scientist, her scatterbrain way to that of pretty woman. However famous Mme du Châtelet may be, she could not be content if she were not celebrated and here, too, she has succeeded, by becoming the declared friend of M. de Voltaire. It is he who gives lustre to her life and it is to him that she will owe her immortality.[5]

The relationship of Mme du Châtelet with Voltaire has always been seen as Mme du Deffand describes it; biographers have seen Mme du Châtelet as one of the characters in the life of the famous man; they have appreciated her influence on him and recognised his distress when she died. And it is probably true that, had she not been Voltaire's mistress, little account would have been taken of Mme du Châtelet. It is only in recent decades that the interest in the Enlightenment in all its manifestations has allowed the contribution of such figures as Mme du Châtelet to be valued in their own right.

In the spring of 1733, the two met, or perhaps met anew – Voltaire claims to remember the young girl from his visits to her parents' salon some fifteen years earlier. Voltaire already had a reputation as the author of *La Henriade* and *L'Histoire de Charles XII*, and above all, as a playwright: *Zaïre* in particular had been a great success in the summer of 1732. He had written, but not published, *Les Lettres anglaises* or *Lettres philosophiques*; in fact although he had the proofs and was adding the letter on Pascal, he was also busy writing to his friends Thierot and Cideville not to bring the book out yet.

Mme du Châtelet's intellectual reputation is reflected in Mme du Deffand's portrait. England and science were interests common to both *philosophes*. Both had read Locke's *Essay on Human Understanding*, both were interested in Newton, whose work was beginning to be discussed in the salons; notably in the salon Mme du Châtelet frequented most often, l'Hôtel Brancas, where Maupertuis, the expert on Newton, was often present. Her knowledge of Latin enabled her to read Newton in the original and, in order to properly understand the work, she was later to ask Maupertuis to help her with the necessary mathematics. Voltaire and Mme du Châtelet seemed destined to become friends.

Early in April of 1733, Mme du Châtelet gave birth to her third child and was told to rest for a few weeks. As soon as she could, she got up and went to the opera with her friend the Duchesse de Saint-Pierre. A friend had taken Voltaire to the box of the Duchesse and he was introduced to her — and to Mme du Châtelet. By 6 May (according to Besterman's dating) Voltaire wrote to her: 'My desire to see you is greater than yours to console me' — he was a state of terror, having to move house. The friendship grew fast and by the beginning of July, Voltaire wrote to his friend, Cideville, 'I dare not send you my poem "to Émilie" on slander because Émilie forbids it'. He was already having to abide by her decisions. Cideville did receive the poem, at least the beginning, copied by a young friend who was staying with Voltaire at the time. The following is a rough translation:

Listen to me, most charming Émilie
You're truly fair; hence half of human kind
Will be your enemy.
Bless'd with a a sublime mind
You will be feared. Your tender friendship
Is full of trust.
Betrayal becomes a must
Your virtue, steady, unwavering,
Simple and unadorned, has brought no offering
To cloaks of piety. Beware of Slander.

After some three months, Voltaire spoke of 'the divine Émilie'
and sent portraits of her to his friends. To Cideville, he wrote:

This is what Émilie is like:
Beautiful; a good friend, too
Imagination blossoming and true
Her mind is lively, nay, sublime
With too much wit some of the time.
She has a genius that is rare
Worthy of Newton, I do swear;
Yet even so she spends her days
With all the world and its petty ways
Playing at cards with gamblers and the like.

And to l'Abbé de Sade:

I'm bound to say she's domineering
And if one wants to get a hearing
It's metaphysics that one has to prove
When the real subject of one's thoughts is love.

The 'divine Émilie' thought he should spend less time on facile
verse; he thought she should spend less time in society. His life
was still that of the bachelor, afraid of his cook, as yet another
rhyme, much quoted, tells:

The other day I entertained
Two goddesses, a friendly pair
The God of love had led them there

> Heavens, Marianne the cook would have been pained
> Had I invited to my lair
> Three guests, the ladies de Saint-Pierre,
> Du Châtelet, M. de Forcalquier
> To stay and partake of *souper*.

The emotional capacity of Mme du Châtelet was as abundant as her energy. While her friendship with Voltaire was blossoming apace in that summer of 1733, she was also very much attracted by the scientist Pierre Louis Moreau de Maupertuis, some eight years her senior (Voltaire was eleven years older). A cavalry lieutenant officer at the age of twenty, his real love was mathematics. He had spent some time in England at the same time as Voltaire and had been made a fellow of the Royal Society while he was there in 1728; the French Académie des Sciences had made him a member some five years earlier. In 1732, he published the first scientific work based on the theories of Newton in French, *Le Discours sur la figure des astres*. Voltaire appreciated his knowledge greatly and asked Maupertuis to check his own brief account of Newton in the *Lettres philosophiques*.[6] Society also appreciated this somewhat reserved scholar and he did not mind the ladies. When he returned from the scientific expedition that went to Lapland to measure the poles and determine their flatness, he brought back two native Lapland women, who added to his fame although they proved a doubtful asset otherwise in Paris.

Maupertuis agreed to help Mme du Châtelet in her mathematical studies. A year later the project was still on: 'M. de Maupertuis thinks that he will be able to teach me geometry', she writes to a friend.[7] She was obviously delighted with her lessons. 'Only with you', she writes to Maupertuis,

> is it a pleasure for me to learn 1a–4a; you strew flowers along a path on which others make one find only nettles, your imagination embellishes the dryest material without taking away any correctness or precision. I am aware how much I would lose if I could not have the benefit of your kindness in condescending to my weakness and teaching me such sublime truths almost playfully.[8]

This flowery style was not one Mme du Châtelet used in her

letters to Maupertuis most of time. Throughout the whole of 1734 she wrote him a series of letters, indicating when she could be found at home, suggesting times for meetings, but mostly expressing her disappointment that he had not come, not written, not sent word of his comings and goings in Paris. She went out of her way to track him down, frequently at the Café Gradot. An amusing anecdote recounts how Mme du Châtelet managed to break the unspoken rule that ladies were not to be served in the main part of the better cafés. Having on one occasion failed to get inside to speak to Maupertuis, to be served, or even to be allowed to sit there, she returned about a week later, dressed in a man's attire. To the delight of Maupertuis and his friends, the management decided not to take too close a look — and served the 'gentleman'.[9]

This persistent pursuit did not detract from her friendship for Voltaire, a friendship that would fairly soon become an acknowledged partnership. There were countless partnerships of the kind which were, on the whole, accepted, although there were degrees of respectability. No one, it seems, objected to the liaison of Voltaire and Mme du Châtelet. It was respectable. The Marquis du Châtelet did not protest and did not mind living under the same roof as Émilie and her poet.[10] For her part she was concerned that her husband should in no way feel affronted. She wrote to her friend, the Duc de Richelieu:

If you see M. du Châtelet, as I have no doubt you will, speak of your esteem and friendship for me; speak especially well of my journey, of my courage and the good impression it makes in society. Speak to him of Voltaire, simply but with concern and friendship and try, in particular, to make him feel that it is madness to be jealous of a wife with whom one is satisfied, whom one esteems and who behaves well. It could be very important for me. He respects your opinion greatly and will easily be of the same mind as you on the matter.[11]

The marquis was concerned for the honour of the family name but he was more than tolerant of the doings of his clever wife and indeed, on one occasion, consoled her, when Voltaire, on an escapade, had betrayed 'us'.

The quasi-marriage relationship between Mme du Châtelet

and Voltaire began with the latter's move to Cirey, the Châtelet estate, in the early summer of 1734. The reason for his going there was a *lettre de cachet* entailing arrest and prison for his *Lettres philosophiques*; the book itself was condemned to public burning on 10 June. Voltaire, who was staying with friends, the Richelieus, was warned by another friend, d'Argental, of the impending *lettre de cachet*. Mme du Châtelet suggested that he go to Cirey, to be out of the way. She would join him there later. And that is what happened. The police was informed by the warrant officer that M. Arouet de Voltaire had left, going, so it is said, to take the waters in Lorraine. The king's order was returned.[12]

Voltaire was duly appreciative and wrote to d'Argental asking if he would, please, 'shut the mouths of anyone he hears speaking ill of a friendship so true and so uncommon'. He settled in and began work furnishing and renovating Cirey. Mme du Châtelet, in the meantime, stayed in Paris to use every influence she had in favour of Voltaire. This did not stop her pursuing Maupertuis, who was currently interested in someone else. Both Mme du Châtelet and Maupertuis were upset but reconciled by a man, who was to become yet another of Mme du Châtelet's teachers and collaborators, Alexis-Claude Clairaut. It was he who now undertook to work with her in her study of geometry.

Like Maupertuis, whom he was to join on the expedition to the pole, Clairaut was a distinguished scientist. At the age of twelve he had presented a memoir to the Académie des Sciences in Paris; at sixteen, he published a mathematical study on curves; and, at eighteen, became a member of the Académie by special dispensation from the king — the minimum age of candidates was twenty. A member of most of the academies in Europe, he was not a socialite and never married. He decided, in fact, never to dine out and when he finally gave in to the importunings of his friends, his stomach could not take it and this, added to a bad cold, led to his death. The *Biographie Universelle* tells how 'La Marquise du Châtelet, wishing to acquire proficiency in mathematics would often go on horseback to visit Clairaut in his retreat for lessons, which gave rise to the work *Les Éléments de géométrie* that he later published'.[13]

By the end of October, Mme du Châtelet finally arrived at Cirey 'surrounded by two hundred packages' and for two months joined in the planning and building — turning most of Voltaire's plans on their heads — before returning to Paris, to a mad life of social distractions. Voltaire dared not show himself yet and had to wait until March 1735 before he was officially told that he could return to the capital, whenever he so wished — which was instantly.

Mme du Châtelet now had to make a serious decision. Voltaire suggested that she choose either Maupertuis and her distractions or life with him in Cirey. She finally opted for the latter: 'I see only the total happiness of curing him of all his fears and spending my life with him', she wrote to the Duc de Richelieu on 21 May, 1735.

The summer of 1735, when they settled in Cirey, was the beginning of a highly productive intellectual life for the couple. They worked together on Newton, on English and German philosophy and on Bible criticism. Practically all Mme du Châtelet's writings were conceived here; here too Voltaire developed the scientific and philosophical content of his work, under the influence of Mme du Châtelet.

The friendship of Voltaire and Mme du Châtelet was now known and generally accepted. The Marquis du Châtelet spent a fair amount of time with the couple at Cirey, and thus lent respectability to the relationship. However all three were concerned to avoid any scandal. This was not always easy, as for instance in the opening stages of a quarrel with l'Abbé Desfontaines, set in the second half of 1735. This literary scandal, a well-known episode in the life of Voltaire, affected Mme du Châtelet strongly and illustrates not only her total involvement but her determination and relentless efforts on behalf of her friend.

Voltaire had written a play, *La Mort de César*, and had allowed it to be performed by students of the Collège d'Harcourt in August. A select audience had been very appreciative. A month later, without the consent or even the knowledge of Voltaire, the play was printed, full of mistakes, amended lines, and even additions. Voltaire, distressed, wrote a letter to Desfontaines, editor of a publication, *Observations*, warning him of the state of the text. Desfontaines who had already written his article, printed it, adding Voltaire's letter, complete with date and address — Cirey. Panic and horror were caused by this indiscretion which could — and did — upset the Marquis du Châtelet. Some of the venom seemed to be taken out of Desfontaines' criticism by a reply defending the text. The reply was written by a friend, Thieriot, and Desfontaines printed it. However, in the meantime, Voltaire sent an aggressive letter on the affair to the famous publication, the *Mercure de France*. Desfontaines was wild and, under the influence of Mme du Châtelet, Voltaire sent him a placating letter, asking for advice on corrections of an edition of his work about to be published in Holland. Desfontaines, in turn, asked for permission to print a recent poem by Voltaire, *l'Épitre à Algarotti*. The poem ends:

> I shall await you
> Quietly admiring your astronomy
> In my meridian, in the fields of Cirey
> Henceforth observing one star only, Émilie,
> And I do swear by lands on which you range
> That her divine charms I will not exchange
> For the equator or the arctic pole.

Voltaire, horrified, stressed the unsuitability, the personal affront implied in making public those private verses. Desfontaines printed them all the same, on 19 November.

Cirey was, temporarily, a most uncomfortable place. The only consolation was that Desfontaines was publicly criticised for publishing another libel — not on Voltaire. Voltaire tended to react either with great friendship or great enmity towards many people. Desfontaines was and remained abhorrent to him — the feeling was reciprocated. One of the other figures involved in the quarrels with Desfontaines was and, as far as Voltaire was concerned, remained a person for whom he was willing to put himself out endlessly and of whom he could not believe any real ill. That person was Thieriot, to whom Voltaire had made a present of the profits of *Les Lettres philosophiques*, whom he had lodged and to whom he had entrusted the printing of several of his writings. Thieriot was not so wholehearted in returning the friendship, claiming that he was also a friend of l'Abbé Desfontaines. Moreover, he regularly kept Prince Frederick of Prussia posted as to the latest reviews, scandals and libels concerning Voltaire. And there was no shortage of these. Mme du Châtelet felt very much involved in all these Voltaire–Desfontaines quarrels. As her correspondence shows, she tried desperately to keep Voltaire calm on the one hand while writing letters full of her indignation and frustration to all her friends, begging them to intervene. The quarrel continued with two publications, both claiming to be written by third parties, each demolishing the work of the 'other' — Desfontaines and Voltaire respectively. Both proved bestsellers in literary society, which followed every move with keen appreciation.

Voltaire had been trying to obtain the censor's approval for his work, *Eléments de la philosophie de Newton*, written at Cirey with the help and encouragement of Mme du Châtelet — he declared the work was really hers. The censors, not at all keen on Newton, delayed giving their consent and in the meantime, a pirated edition was printed in Holland, once again full of errors, misprints and even additions — a gift to anyone wishing to find fault with it. The title page read *Eléments de la philosophie de Newton mis à la portée de tout le monde* (put within the reach of every one). This, Desfontaines said, should read 'mis à la porte de tout le monde' (shown the door by everyone). Voltaire replied with one of his little rhymes sent to Thieriot, that is, sent the rounds in Paris. Desfontaines in turn duly ridiculed Voltaire's love of Newton. Voltaire replied with a pamphlet, *Le Préservatif contre les observations*, which appeared under the name of the Chevalier de Mouhy, picking on every mistake the *Observations* had ever been guilty of and heaping ridicule on Desfontaines whom he also accused of ingratitude for past help. Within a month, December 1738, Desfontaines responded with *La Voltairomanie ou Lettre d'un jeune avocat*, denouncing Voltaire's work as dangerous and even blasphemous, so that decent people did not wish to associate with the author and such that Voltaire dared not live in Paris. As for the accusation of ingratitude, this, he claimed, was based on Voltaire's pique about an alleged pamphlet supposedly written by Desfontaines after his release from prison — with Voltaire's help — and apparently burnt by Thieriot. Desfontaines claimed there was never any such pamphlet. Within two weeks, two thousand copies were sold of *La Voltairomanie*.

Two copies arrived in Cirey at the end of 1738. Mme du Châtelet was horrified when she saw hers and was determined that Voltaire should not see it. She wrote to her friend d'Argental,

Sir Isaac Newton, *ca* 1726, by an unknown artist (detail)

Mme du Châtelet with Francesco Algarotti,
from the frontispiece of *Il Newtonianismo per le dame*,
F. Algarotti, Naples, 1737

The terrible state of health of your friend made me decide to take any risk rather than let him be acquainted with that terrible libel of Desfontaines or with anything else against him. I must confess to you that when I saw a large packet from La Marre whose handwriting I know, I removed it and opened it. In it I found the infamous libel and a letter that would have killed your friend. . . . I have thrown de La Marre's letter into the fire.[14]

This well-intentioned act of protectiveness had an awkward side to it. The packet also contained the text of Voltaire's play, *L'Envieux*, which she could not hand to him without saying that she had opened his mail. If he found out, he would, she feared no longer trust her. Fortunately for her, Voltaire had other worries. A copy of *La Voltairomanie* did reach him and he was concerned to keep it from her! Voltaire decided on criminal proceedings. Mme du Châtelet wrote to everybody, including Frederick of Prussia. In the end Desfontaines dissociated himself from *La Voltairomanie* and Voltaire did the same for *Le Préservatif*.

All this time Mme du Châtelet and Voltaire did not halt their studies and writings. They welcomed guests who shared their interests, such as the charming young Francesco Algarotti, son of a rich Venetian merchant. Algarotti was travelling round Europe to learn French and English. Mme du Châtelet called him marquis, though he was not. He, too, was interested in Newton and while all three were 'Newtonising', he worked on his dialogues popularising Newton for ladies, *Il Newtonianismo per le dame*. No difficult mathematics were presented. 'I have tried', he wrote, 'to make my book interesting, in much the same way that plays are; can there be anything in the world, especially if one is addressing ladies, where the interest of the heart are lost sight of?'[15] There is one passage, Mme du Châtelet tells her friend Maupertuis, where he says that love decreases in inverse ratio to absence and to cubed distance and, according to his first proposition, a lover who has not seen his mistress for eight days loves her sixty-four times less![16] Algarotti's hopes were that there might one day be a happy society in which English good sense could be linked to French delicateness and Italian imagination.

Algarotti stayed at Cirey twice, at the end of 1735 and at the end of 1736. His work proved popular, a translation into French appearing in 1738. Mme du Châtelet had rather expected the book to be dedicated to her — indeed that must have been the original intention, judging by the fact that her portrait is the frontispiece of the 1737 edition.[17] To her chagrin, Algarotti changed his mind and dedicated the work to Fontenelle — most unsuitable, Mme du Châtelet thought, Fontenelle deserved philosophical homage but not that of figuring at the head of a work on Newton whose professed enemy he was.

Other work was not neglected; work on the English deists, Mme du Châtelet's translation of Mandeville's *The Fable of the Bees*, the daily Bible text sessions where she and Voltaire both made notes on which each later based their works on the Bible; Mme du Châtelet developed her notes into *L'Examen de la Genèse* and *l'Examen des livres du Nouveau Testament*. There was also work on the nature of fire. The Académie des Sciences had set as prize subject in 1736, the topic *La Nature du feu et sa propagation*; entries had to be in by 1 September, 1737. Voltaire decided to enter and proceeded to set up experiments in his laboratory, weighing metals, wood, vegetables before and after combustion, noting that nothing definite could be proved as to the weight of fire; the same objects would sometimes lose and sometimes gain weight in his experiments. Mme du Châtelet watched all the experiments with interest and, one month before the date of entry, decided to enter the competition herself. She kept this a secret, worked by night, sleeping for only one hour and keeping herself awake by plunging her hands in iced water, pacing up and down and beating her arms. She wrote to Maupertuis:

> I believe you will have been very surprised that I was bold enough to write a memoir for the Académie. I wanted to try out my ability incognito. . . . M. du Châtelet was the only one I took into my confidence and he kept my secret so well that he said nothing to you in Paris. I was unable to carry out any experiment because I was working without M. de Voltaire knowing about it and I would not have been able to hide them from him. . . . I did not tell M. de Voltaire because I did not wish to have to blush about an undertaking that might have displeased him. Moreover, I opposed almost all his ideas in my work; I did not confess until I saw in the gazette that neither he nor I had a share in the prize![18]

She explained to Maupertuis that her memoir established that fire had no weight and could be something which, like space, was neither abstract not material: 'I do not think that this idea cannot be defended, however singular it may at first sight appear.'

Although neither was awarded the prize, both memoirs were printed together with those of the winners. Mme du Châtelet quotes a letter to Voltaire from M. de Réaumur: 'It is imperative that the public should know that among the submissions for the prize on the nature of fire there was one by a young woman and another by the greatest of our poets.'[19] The Académie decided that the curiosity of the public would be aroused by the names of these two competitors. 'Submission no. 6 is by a lady of high rank, Mme la Marquise du Chastellet and no. 7 by one of our best poets'.[20]

Mme du Châtelet was of course, disappointed: 'It is hard that the prize should have been shared and that M. de Voltaire had none of the cake. I am sure that the M. Fuller [really Euler] named is a Leibnizian, consequently a Cartesian.'[21]

Until the quarrel with Desfontaines blew up, Voltaire and Mme du Châtelet were happy:

> Comforts and luxuries both I love
> Paradise on earth is where I am.

was Voltaire's verdict in *Le Mondain*. Mme du Châtelet put herself out endlessly to please him. She spared no effort, omitted no frivolity, wrote Mme Denis, Voltaire's niece, after a visit to Cirey in the spring of 1738: 'there is no passage from the best philosophers that she does not recite to him. A woman of great intellect, she is also very pretty and uses every art to seduce him. Voltaire is more enchanted than ever.'[22]

Mme du Châtelet was happy while Voltaire was in her company at Cirey. But she suffered, apparently, from an underlying feeling of insecurity which made her panic every time Voltaire set off anywhere else on his own. 'The journey to Paris will make me die. In the name of God, spare me the cruel despair,' she wrote to her friend d'Argental, 'you can surely persuade him',[23] and when Voltaire went to Berlin she was ill with anxiety: 'I have a fever and I hope soon to end like that poor Mme de Richelieu' (who had recently died).[24] Voltaire travelled either because things were too hot for him in France (*Le Mondain*, *La Pucelle* circulated well before they were in print) or because he was tempted by persistent invitations from the Crown Prince Frederick, later King of Prussia.

The first time he set off to the Netherlands he was almost as upset as she was. 'When I see the moment arrive when I have to leave for ever someone who has done everything for me, who has for me left Paris, all her friends and all the pleasures of her life, a person I worship and am bound to worship. . . the situation is horrible.'[25] Nonetheless, he did go. And although he returned, especially when she pleaded that she was dying, it was not always gladly. The court of Frederick was very attractive intellectually and he felt very flattered by the admiration of the king. Frederick did not extend his invitations to Mme du Châtelet. She was fully aware of all this, which only heightened her anxiety. Her relationship with Frederick was never very warm. They exchanged letters but each wished the other did not exist. Frederick sent gifts to her and to Voltaire which she invariably acknowledged; she sent him her *Institutions de physique* and received in return a letter full of praise with just enough criticism to make it credible. She missed no occasion to pay him her respects, such as wishing him a Happy New Year; occasionally she asked if he would intervene, usually to help Voltaire, as in the Desfontaines quarrel. When there was talk that he might pay a visit to France, she hastened to extend an invitation:

> M. de Valory [the Ambassador of France in Prussia] has told M. de Voltaire and the *Gazettes* almost announce that your Majesty will honour France with your presence. I am not trying to discover whether the minister and the gazeteer are right, but I dare to represent to your Majesty that Cirey is on your way and that I would never console myself if I did not have the honour of receiving your person here where we have so often paid our homage.[26]

When Voltaire returned from Berlin, Mme du Châtelet was more than relieved, as she wrote to d'Argental: 'The King of Prussia is astonished that one can leave him to go to Brussels [where she was]. . . . There is nothing he did not do to keep your friend [Voltaire]. I believe he is outraged against me, but I defy him to

32

hate me more than I have hated him for the last two months.'[27]

Her fears were justified to a certain extent. In 1743, Voltaire spent five months in Prussia and she was beside herself not only at his being with Frederick, but at his seeming lack of haste to return. Nevertheless like a good 'wife', she took a positive line:

What I have endured in the last month would detach any other person but, although he can' make me unhappy, he cannot make me less sensitive and I feel that I shall never be reasonable. I would not want to be, even if it were in my power and, in spite of all my suffering, I am really persuaded that the one who loves best is still the happiest.[28]

The couple also travelled together. In particular, they went to Belgium (May 1739) where Mme du Châtelet hoped to settle a long-standing law-suit over a property for her husband. Neither intended to interrupt current studies just because they were not in Cirey. They packed books, took their servants and set off in two coaches, accompanied by a young Swiss mathematician, Koenig. Mme du Châtelet had asked him to teach her algebra for three hours a day; she also planned to spend three further hours daily on 'homework'. They travelled without haste, stopped for picnics and were welcomed in many towns with pomp and circumstance. There was a performance of a Voltaire play, a banquet, a ballet. The property in Beringhen, near Liège, proved not at all welcoming and they spent as little time there as possible. They went on to Brussels where they rented a comfortable house in the Rue de la Grosse-Tour. Voltaire worked on *Le Siècle de Louis XIV* and on *Mahomet*. Mme du Châtelet began a translation of *Oedipus* by Sophocles. She also listened to law lectures, so that she could understand the law-suit; she set about learning Flemish; and she worked with Koenig, who had been recommended to her by Maupertuis. 'I have so little leisure for myself that that I have no time to know whether life is gay or sad in Brussels.'[29]

The lessons were a mixed success. Koenig was a disciple of the German philosophers Leibniz and Wolff, and his lessons were as much on philosophy as on algebra. Mme du Châtelet was genuinely interested and decided to preface her work on Newton, *Institutions de physique*, with a section devoted to German metaphysical theories. Somewhat unsure of herself, she intended the book to be published anonymously and to own it if it met with approval. To her dismay, Koenig not only divulged the name of the author, but claimed that the work was in fact his. Mme du Châtelet's account of the story was given to another young mathematician who, she hoped, would take the place of Koenig, who had now left, disgruntled.

> I hesitated for a long time before, at last, I confided my secret [the authorship] to him, finally convinced of his integrity and loyalty. I found it an advantage to be able to read my work to a clever man and to be sure, consequently, that there were no mistakes, which I expected since I had not consulted anyone; also that of having the help of his knowledge in my plan to set at the front of my work some of the ideas of M. Leibniz on metaphysics. At about that time we were leaving for Paris. More than half the book was printed; I asked the publisher to re-set the pages on which I wished to have my new metaphysics and to have some galleys and I set to work. To do it well, I had to read several chapters of the works of Wolff, e.g. on ontology, cosmology etc. . . as well as his metaphysics which I had read and which I had with me. I didn't have time to look for the ideas I needed in big quarto volumes. I begged M. Koenig to make extracts for me of the chapters I required, which he was kind enough to do and on this I partly based my work. I left to come here, having arranged everything and with my secret which had not been leaked in two years. I thus saw myself on the verge of enjoying the pleasure of an incognito; but no sooner had I left than M. de Koenig told everyone, adding that I had written a book that was worth nothing, that he had made me write another and that I had not paid him enough for his trouble. Imagine the noise that that caused; it reached me and I was outraged.[30]

An account written much later by Formey, who was working for Voltaire, gives a somewhat different picture. According to this version Koenig came to every session with Mme du Châtelet armed with a paper, on which the particular 'lesson' he wished to expound was written. He would proceed to explain and prove. He would then ask Mme du Châtelet whether she understood and accepted it. If the answer was yes, he would present the paper to her, saying 'sign'. According to Formey, the signed papers provided the material for the *Institutions de physique*.[31]

There would seem to be some truth in both accounts. Koenig clearly did provide the material, not for the whole work, much of which was already in print, but for the first section which set out to explain German metaphysics to the French reader.

When the book was ready, Mme du Châtelet sent a copy to Frederick of Prussia who wrote back in flattering terms which yet could be understood to put the author in her place, expressing his amazement that the work of a profound German metaphysician could have been translated and refashioned 'by a gracious French lady'.[32] Frederick was not really impressed and, to others, wrote that the work was by a woman who meddled in writing things she had not digested and 'when one tries to explain things one does not understand oneself', it is 'like a stammerer trying to teach a mute to speak'.[33]

At all events, Koenig left and Mme du Châtelet had difficulty finding someone else to help her with her studies. Maupertuis, who had recommended Koenig to her, was not keen to see any repetition of the embarrassment caused. He therefore dissuaded another young scientist friend of his, the Swiss Johann Bernoulli, from taking on Koenig's position, much to Mme du Châtelet's chagrin.

The law-suit in Belgium dragged on for several years and, when it was finally won, Mme du Châtelet was anxious to dispose of the disputed property. Brussels, they found, was not particularly stimulating and they travelled about, spending time in Paris, and briefly at Cirey. Voltaire went to Prussia.

They returned to Paris for the summer of 1739, where the marriage of Louise Elisabeth de Bourbon to the son of Phillip V of Spain, Philippe de Bourbon, provided a whirl of social life and excitement.

Although they spent a great deal of time with their hosts, the Richelieus — the Duchesse de Richelieu was seriously ill with a very difficult pregnancy — Mme de Châtelet and Voltaire also watched the fireworks and attended an endless round of suppers. Voltaire found it all too much and became ill; Mme du Châtelet had a much stronger constitution. The fare was of high quality no doubt, as regards food; it certainly was in intellectual terms, their fellow guests being distinguished scientists — such as Mairan with whom Mme du Châtelet had a lively, rather public controversy on 'les forces vives' (kinetic energy), Fontenelle, permanent secretary of the Académie and the young philosopher Helvétius, to name but a few.

Voltaire and Mme du Châtelet returned to Paris in 1741 and 1742. Mme du Châtelet rented a house in the Faubourg Saint-Honoré in which Voltaire occupied the first floor. This time Mme du Châtelet pressurised her friends in society to help Voltaire at court which was not easy Frederick's known friendship with Voltaire did not help. The King of Prussia, anxious to have Voltaire at his own court, took some trouble to have him discredited in Paris, by such ploys as putting about a letter, disowned but in fact probably written by Voltaire to Frederick, saying: 'You are no longer our ally, Sire, but you will become the ally of mankind' (France sought an alliance with Frederick against Austria but Frederick was in the process of signing a peace treaty with Austria). The letter also referred to 'the old man, Fleury', Cardinal Fleury, who was Mme du Châtelet's trump contact in her campaign for Voltaire. Various society houses were rumoured to have closed their doors to Voltaire. 'Mme du Châtelet must be in a fine state of anxiety' wrote Mme du Deffand. She was indeed in 'a fine state of anxiety' but her diplomatic efforts prevented any serious consequences, for a time.

However, she did not always win. Voltaire's play *Mahomet*, which had a few initial very successful performances, was denounced as impious, anti-religious, anti-Christian. The chief of police sent for Voltaire who, although already in bed, immediately set off, together with Mme du Châtelet, and agreed to withdraw the play. The couple once again left Paris, somewhat abruptly. They did not stay away long, however, since Voltaire was hoping to become one of the forty 'immortals', a member of the Académie Française. Mme du Châtelet worked hard on her friends but, twice, Voltaire failed to get elected. Her protector Cardinal Fleury had died and she now tried her best with the new minister, Maurepas, but in vain; Voltaire went to Prussia and stayed away for five months. She was, briefly, very happy when he returned at the end of 1743, but the happiness did not last and, by 1744, the couple were not as united as they had been. In Paris and at Versailles, Mme du Châtelet spent some time working to advance the position of her children; she wished for a post of chancellor in the queen's household for her youngest and she married her daughter off to the wealthy Duke of Montenero-

Caraffa. She lived the society life — and lost large sums of money at cards.

Voltaire had lent her considerable sums, but he now insisted on repayments and he ensured that his finances were kept separate from hers. The young Helvétius, friend and *philosophe* but also tax-farmer, insisted on having all outstanding debts paid up and threatened to send in the bailiffs. Voltaire fell in love, briefly, with an actress, Mlle Gaussin, a great *Zaïre*, and the Marquis du Châtelet wished to have his wife back home. Altogether it was not a happy situation.

In the summer of 1744, Mme du Châtelet and Voltaire were back at Cirey. Voltaire was working on *La Princesse de Navarre*, a comédie-ballet intended for the wedding festivities of the Dauphin to the Infanta of Spain. He and Rameau were commissioned by the Duc de Richelieu and although Voltaire took endless trouble over it, he was constantly being asked to amend and change. As so often, the pressure made him ill and Mme du Châtelet was more than worried. She wrote to d'Argental:

> I beg you to give your approval this time and to keep the criticism for another occasion. I promise to make any corrections you want, but if you appear dissatisfied and overwhelm him with criticism, you will make him die. His health is in an appalling state, he is upset, he is worried, he forced himself to work and has given himself a fever. . . .If in that state, you give him new work and new fears that his work will not be approved, you will make him die, and me, too, as a result.[34]

Mme du Châtelet's anxiety and her concern for Voltaire were genuine and in spite of some strained relations between the two, the friendship — Mme du Châtelet began to speak in terms of her 'friendship' for her 'companion' — remained unshaken. And to the outside world, all was bliss. When the President Hénault, president of the chamber and friend of the queen, payed a visit to Cirey, he reported back on their life of pleasure and Mme du Châtelet wrote of the delightful session they had weeping over a Voltaire text.[35]

Mme du Châtelet was also working, mainly on a translation of Newton's *Principia Mathematica* from Latin. As usual, she consulted experts, corresponding now with the Jesuit scholar, Le

Père François Jacquier, who had a chair in biblical studies, but had also published a joint commentary on Newton with a colleague and was to hold chairs in physics and mathematics in Rome. As well as this work, she embarked on her *Discours sur le bonheur*, a reflection, Vaillot believes, of her changing relationship with Voltaire.

Their stay at Cirey was not a long one. Mme du Châtelet and Voltaire were still needed in Brussels and they went to Paris for two important occasions: in September, to celebrate the king's recovery; in November, for his return to the city. A much reported anecdote tells how Mme du Châtelet, Voltaire and their host, De Champs, were in a carriage in the midst of the festivities; the streets were so crowded that no carriage could move. Mme du Châtelet, covered in diamonds as was her wont, climbed out of the carriage, shouting for help, and strode through into the drinking and brawling crowd, her two friends presumably following her. They happened to be near the house of the President Hénault, who was away. Undeterred, Mme du Châtelet sent for a roast chicken and all three had an enjoyable meal, toasting the health of their absent friend in his house, 'where everyone would like to see you back'.[36]

In the mid-1740s Voltaire enjoyed success. He was appointed Royal Historiographer, the court smiled on him; even the Pope seemed to welcome the dedication of *Mahomet*, and he was finally elected to the Académie (1746), to Mme du Châtelet's delight. Voltaire's niece, Mme Denis, recently widowed, was proving a great attraction and he spent much time in her house. Mme du Châtelet was not aware of the extent to which Voltaire was fond of his niece, but she sensed the cooling relationship; her emphasis, in 1745, on the merit of friendship, once love is no longer possible, in *Discours sur le Bonheur* may reflect her effort to accept the situation. She also stressed the vital importance, for women, of a love of study, which would compensate for all they have to endure as women. She accordingly worked persistently on her translation of Newton.

Mme du Châtelet and Voltaire now spent a great deal of time at court. They had an apartment at Versailles, a place in Paris — they moved to Rue Traversière — and they occasionally stayed with friends such as De Champs. Mme du Châtelet, inevitably, provided splendid material for the gossip-rounds. One example was her trip to Fontainebleau with the court, going in the queen's entourage. Three carriages stood ready to take the ladies. The queen got into the first one, Mme du Châtelet jumped into the second, thereby shocking the other noble ladies who refused to join her; they stepped into the third carriage and then refused to allow her to join them. Such gaffes were typical of her impetuous and rather eccentric behaviour. Another instance which figures in Longchamp's *Voltaire et Mme du Châtelet* was Mme du Châtelet's summer outing together with a number of society ladies among whom the Marquise de Meuse, the Marquise de Boufflers, Mme du Deffand (author of the cruel pen-portrait of Mme du Châtelet), Mme de Graffigny and Mme de la Popelinière are named. Mme du Châtelet had ordered a supper in advance and the group set off in their carriages. They clearly enjoyed their picnic, 'wearing hardly any clothing', 'laughing and singing until five o'clock in the morning, when the carriages called for them, the servants having thoughtfully sent mantles'.[37]

Yet Mme du Châtelet was accepted and, it would seem, liked. The Royal privilege for her work on Newton, granted on 1746, long before the work was complete, reads: 'Our well-beloved Mme la Marquise du Châtelet has indicated to us that she wishes to have printed and to offer to the public a work of translation by herself, bearing the title *'Principes mathématiques de la philosophie naturelle.* . . . Louis by the grace of God, King of France and of Navarre'.

At the same time, her scholarship was gaining recognition, at least in Italy where the Bologna Institute made her a member. It was not the sort of thing that could happen in France, as her friend, Cideville wrote:

> When Bologna proudly displays, in Italy
> Its register adorned with the fair name of Émilie
> Why is the fair sex, so greatly loved by us,
> Excluded, in France, from the Academy?[38]

Mme du Châtelet wrote to Jacquier, telling him how flattered she was by the honour, how pleased to owe it to his friendship and how delighted she would be to have her new title set at the top of her work on Newton. As usual, she intended to participate fully in the life around her and yet manage her work:

You must know that I lead the most disorganised life, that I am spending my days in the ante-chamber of the minister for war in order to obtain a regiment for my son, that I go to bed at four or five in the morning and that I am working on a translation of Newton whenever I have time... my work, which is nearly complete, is still a secret and I commend it to you.[39]

The work still required a great deal of time, in fact. By the end of 1746, she was still urgently asking for a copy of Jacquier's commentary on Newton.[40] By April, 1747, she was reading proofs of the translation and working on the commentary, she tells Jacquier.[41] It was to occupy her intellectually until her death, two and a half years later. She was helped in her work by Clairaut, who checked the translation and whose own commentary was, in part, incorporated into the work. The publisher advised the public that full confidence could be placed in the book 'since it is work of the late Madame la Marquise du Chastellet', whom he termed 'the illustrious interpreter' and since it had been checked by M. Clairaut.[42] Voltaire, whose interest and encouragement were always at her service, was delighted that 'Mme Newton-Pompom du Châtelet' had outgrown her interest in Leibniz and his monads and regained her proper evaluation of scientific truths.

Voltaire was less delighted with Mme du Châtelet's new emotional involvement, in these last years. The couple were restless. They payed two visits to the Duchesse du Maine at Anet-Sceaux, and Mme du Châtelet threw herself into acting in Voltaire's plays, at Anet and at Circy, when they were there. Both were rather pleased, early in 1748, to accept an invitation to the court of Stanislas Leczszinski, at Lunéville.[43] More acting, more festivities and a handsome young court poet, Saint-Lambert.

Mme du Châtelet had had a passing fancy, or so it is assumed, for a certain Charlier, the lawyer involved in the Belgian litigation, now happily concluded; the only indication of this particular fancy are the terms of endearment, such as 'dear angel' which recur in her letters to him, 'angel' being otherwise used by her only when writing to the d'Argentals. Now that the relationship with Voltaire was on strictly 'friendship' terms, she fell hopelessly in love with the young poet at Lunéville. She was forty-two and he, ten years younger. He was to go down in history not for his poetry but because of his affair, then, with Voltaire's official mistress and later, on account of his being the official lover of Mme d'Houdetot with whom Jean-Jacques Rousseau had fallen passionately in love. At the time he was one of a string of lovers of the clever and beautiful Mme de Boufflers, herself the accredited mistress of King Stanislas. While Saint-Lambert at first responded to the advances of Mme du Châtelet, he apparently soon cooled off, as her countless letters to him testify. As in the early friendship with Maupertuis, she constantly complained that he did not write and seemed distant. She sent him gifts and asked him to write verses for her; she let herself go and endlessly analysed his and her reactions. She found briefly that she could work properly 'on my Newton, which is, to me a highly precious and most essential task'.[44] She could not bear to be away even for a short time, in Paris, in Cirey, or at Plombières where she had been sent to take the waters with Mme de Boufflers — and to act as the latter's 'chaperone'. However, much of the year was spent at Lunéville or in Stanislas' other residence, Commercy.

Longchamp, Voltaire's secretary, who had joined the Châtelet household in 1746,[45] reports that one day Voltaire, unexpectedly entering the rooms of Mme du Châtelet, found her with Saint-Lambert in what was clearly an unequivocal situation. His fury and threats to leave were apparently appeased by Mme du Châtelet who followed him out of the room and explained that she was concerned for his health and, given her own temperament, had thought that a friend of Voltaire's would provide the best solution. . . . Voltaire, it seems, was satisfied, especially as this allowed him greater freedom to pay attention to his niece.

The real trouble began at Cirey, in January 1749, when Mme du Châtelet told Voltaire that she was pregnant. They sent for Saint-Lambert and all three plotted to make the Marquis du Châtelet appear as the father. And they succeeded. They persuaded him to come to attend to some legal matters and, during his six-week stay, he was, writes Longchamp, 'seduced by his wife' who then told him that he was to be a father again, which pleased him. Mme du Châtelet was very conscious of her situation. She wrote to Mme de Boufflers to enlist her help: 'I am pregnant and you can imagine the distressing state I am in, how much I fear for my health, even for my life, how ridiculous I find it to be giving birth at the age of forty, not having had children for the last seventeen years, how upset I am for my son.'[46]

She very much wanted the birth to take place at Lunéville and asked Mme de Boufflers to find out whether that would be 'possible and suitable'. In the event, King Stanislas was most kind and allowed her the little house she wished for. Her son reacted as she had expected and by May she was writing to Saint-Lambert: 'I am less pleased with my son; I am not sure whether he loves me as much as he should. He did not take my pregnancy very well.'[47] Most of the time, her one concern was to be assured of Saint-Lambert's affection and she wrote him letter after letter: 'I think I would write to you the whole day and the whole night, if I did not fear it would be too much for you; all other occupations are very dull in comparison.'[48]

She was full of forebodings, desperate to finish her book before the birth which might well, she repeatedly stated, cost her her life. 'My affliction and despondency would frighten me if I believed in forebodings', she wrote in her last letter to Saint-Lambert. To l'Abbé Claude Sallier, of the King's Library, she wrote, on 1 September, 1749:

I am taking the liberty you have allowed me to place in your hands some manuscripts I am most interested to have preserved. I very much hope that I shall be able to thank you for your kindness and that my labour which I am expecting at any time, will not be as fatal as I fear. I beg of you to set numbers to these manuscripts and to have them registered, so that they do not get lost — M. de Voltaire, who is here with me sends you his tenderest compliments.

The letter accompanied the first volume of her work on Newton. Voltaire was indeed with her, having faithfully, if somewhat reluctantly, accompanied her to Lorraine and to Circy.

Saint-Lambert was also there much of the time, as were Mme de Boufflers and her husband. On 4 September, Voltaire wrote to d'Argenson:

Mme du Châtelet informs you, Sir, that this night, being at her desk and scribbling a notice about Newton, she felt a little call.

The little call was a daughter, who appeared in the instant. She was laid on a quarto tome of geometry. The mother has gone to lie down because one must needs lie down and, if she were not asleep, she would be writing to you.

The child was handed over to a wet nurse and all seemed to be well for the next few days. That particular autumn was apparently very hot and, on 9 September, Mme du Châtelet, suffering from the heat, insisted on being given an ice cold drink. This led to an attack of suffocation which looked serious. She did seem to respond to medication and asked for the manuscript of her commentary on Newton, adding the date, 10 September, 1749. A little later, she lost consciousness and died before her friends, hastily summoned from dinner with Mme de Boufflers, could reach her bedside. Voltaire was terribly upset and fainted on leaving the room. Longchamp relates that Mme de Boufflers asked him to remove a ring from the dead woman's hand. It had, inside, the portrait of Saint-Lambert, which Mme de Boufflers removed, sending the ring on to the Marquis du Châtelet. Longchamp told Voltaire of the incident and he apparently replied 'just like women. I had replaced Richelieu. Saint-Lambert drove me out. One nail drives out another. That is the way of the world'.[49]

The obituary in Grimm's *Correspondance littéraire*[50] was not fulsome in its praise, speaking of a lady, who 'so famous in foreign lands, had here more critics than partisans'. Her friend and scientific mentor, Maupertuis appreciated her true merit, and wrote:

Society is losing a noble and pleasant figure of a woman who is rightly regretted, the more so because, having great wit, she never put it to bad use. . . .How marvellous, besides, to have been able to ally the pleasing qualities of her sex with that sublime science which we believe to be meant only for us. This surprising feat will make her memory for ever respected.[51]

Notes

1. René Vaillot, *Madame du Châtelet*, p. 23. The Marquise de Créqui had let it be known that Gabrielle Émilie was born in 1702 and was really older than she made herself out to be.
2. Maurice Cousin, *Souvenirs de la Marquise de Créqui*, 1834–7, 7 vols (vol. 1).
3. R. Vaillot, *Madame du Châtelet*, p. 44.
4. Maurepas, *Mémoires*, Paris, 1792, vol. iv, p. 173, quoted in *Lettres de la Marquise du Châtelet*,(ed.) Th. Besterman, vol. 1, pp. 11–12.
5. *Lettres de la Marquise du Châtelet*, (ed.) Th. Besterman, vol. 1, pp. 13–14, based on a manuscript copy. Several versions of this famous portrait were in circulation. The one printed in Grimm's *Correspondance littéraire* (March 1777) is rather more crude.
6. Letters 14–17 in Voltaire's *Lettres philosophiques*.
7. Letter to l'Abbé de Sade, 15 July 1734.
8. Letter of 7 June 1734.
9. S. Edwards, *The Divine Mistress*, p. 64.
10. M. Pellison, *Les Hommes de lettres au 18ème siècle*, p. 180.
11. Letter of 22 May 1735.
12. Vaillot, *Madame du Châtelet*, p. 92.
13. *Biographie universelle* (Michaud), entry on Clairaut.
14. Letter of 29 December 1738.
15. F. Algarotti, *Il Newtonianismo per le dame*, author's preface.
16. Letter of 3 September 1738.
17. *Il Newtonianismo per le dame*, engraving by Marco Pitteri; cf. *Lettres de la Marquise du Châtelet*, (ed.) Besterman, vol. 1, p. 114 note.
18. Letter of 21 June [1738].
19. Letter of 7 July [1738].
20. Ibid.
21. Letter of 22 May [1738].
22. F. Hamel, *An Eighteenth-Century Marquise*, p. 165.
23. Letter of 5 February [1739].
24. Letter to Duc de Richelieu, 23 November [1740].
25. Letter of 9 December 1736.
26. Letter to Frederick, 11 August 1740.
27. Letter to d'Argental, 7 January 1741.
28. Letter of 22 October 1743.
29. Letter to Maupertuis, 20 June [1739].
30. Letter to Johann Bernoulli [30 June, 1740].
31. Vaillot, *Madame du Châtelet*, p. 184; J.-H. Formey, *Souvenirs d'un citoyen*.
32. Letter of 19 May 1740.
33. Letter to Jordan, 24 September 1740.
34. Letter of 10 July 1744.
35. Note to letter of 8 July [1744].
36. Vaillot, *Madame du Châtelet*, p. 263.

37. Cf. Hamel, *An Eighteenth-Century Marquise*, pp. 126–7; Vaillot, *Madame du Châtelet*, p. 264.
38. Vaillot, ibid., p. 263.
39. Letter of 12 November 1745.
40. Letter to Johann Bernoulli, 6 September 1746.
41. Letter of 13 April 1747.
42. Publisher's notice to *Principes mathématiques*.
43. Cf. p. 3 of the present volume.
44. Letter of 5 June 1748.
45. Cf. Longchamp, *Voltaire et Mme du Châtelet*, (eds.) Albanès and Harvard.
46. Letter of 3 April 1749.
47. Letter of 3 May [1749].
48. Letter of [April 1749].
49. Voltaire's real feelings commemorating his mistress, were expressed in his 'Eulogy' later published as the preface to her work on Newton; it is translated below in full in the Appendix.
50. Grimm, *Correspondance littéraire*, vol. 1, 1749.
51. E. Badinter, *Émilie, Émilie*, pp. 467–8.

3 The Writings of Mme du Châtelet

Mme du Châtelet's works reflect her range of interests, her personality and the role she saw as hers in society. Her learning and research, her passion for knowledge, if possible scientific and logical knowledge combined, is evident in her books on Leibniz and on Newton and also in the brief text on grammar. Her concern for society comes through in her rendering of Mandeville's *The Fable of the Bees*. A certain humility made her see her own intellectual contribution as helping to make the work of others accessible either by accounts of their ideas or by translations. Finally, her love of life and her need for self-fulfilment made her search for possible sources of happiness in the *Discours sur le bonheur*. In all this she was very conscious of being a woman, just as she was aware of the privileged position she held in society. Imbued with a strong sense of service to society, she made a powerful plea that other women should be offered similar opportunities, so that the time might come when 'a good tragedy, a good poem, a respected tale, a fine painting' might be the work of a woman; the last item on her list, 'a good book on physics' was realised — she wrote it herself!

Leibniz and Newton

Les Institutions physiques, later *Institutions de physique*, received the approbation of the censor in 1738. The publisher's notice to the first edition states that it was printed in Paris in 1740 and that the additions on the metaphysics of Mr Leibniz delayed the printing.

The book originally intended to explain the work of Newton. During the time Mme du Châtelet was writing, the world of scholarship was divided between the systems of Descartes and Newton. And since Descartes had been adequately expounded, it was Newton she wanted to present, giving her account a wider scope than the recently published *Eléments de la philosophie de*

Newton by Voltaire. And indeed, of the twenty chapters of her book more than half seem to be concerned with science, with matter, gravity, weight, equilibrium of forces and the like. But by the time the work was complete, her interest had shifted and chapters on the divisibility of matter, on inertia and dynamic force show philosophical argument as having as much relevance as scientific description.

What she wanted, as she explains in her foreword, was to find a form of calculation in metaphysics similar to that offered by geometry, by means of which, given certain data, it would become possible to resolve a range of unknowns. 'It is certain', she writes, 'that there are a number of points in metaphysics which lend themselves to demonstrations just as rigorous as the demonstrations of geometry, even if they are different in kind.'

When the book was published, she sent a copy to Frederick of Prussia and, forgetting all about Newton, wrote:

> My plan is to set out a whole philosophy in the manner of Mr Wolff, but with a French sauce. I shall try to make the sauce a short one. I think we lack such a work. The works of Mr Wolff would rebut the frivolous French mind, if only by their form, but I am convinced that my compatriots will appreciate the precise and rigorous reasoning, once they are no longer frightened by words like lemmas, theorems, proofs, which seem out of place when they are used outside geometry.[1]

Notices and reviews of the *Institutions* speak of her remarkably clear exposition of German philosophy, not of the chapters devoted to Newton.

Leibniz in the Institutions de physique

The interrelationship between science and metaphysics — physics and metaphysics as it was termed — as also between ethics and religion was hotly debated in the rationalist climate of eighteenth-century France. The *philosophes* were more or less agreed that morality and religion had to be separated. The belief that right and wrong could have been determined by revelation was not acceptable to the rational mind. Turning to philosophy which, in the early years of the century still included scientific knowledge, the *philosophes* were conscious that reason could not attain the kind of certain knowledge about the universe which empirical knowledge provided about the world around us. The tendency, therefore, was to separate these two domains as well. As far as Voltaire was concerned, morality could be determined by a study of man as a social animal, while science provided an account of the physical habitat of man. Man was thus enabled to understand how he and the world functioned, though not why man and the universe are as they are. Just as to know how a clock functions does not answer the question as to what purpose it serves.

Questions of this kind led to reasoned enquiries in three directions, each of which was pursued by one of the great writers of the day. They had a common starting-point — man's existence. For Voltaire, the quest led from there to a creator, whose existence the mind can grasp, but whose relationship with what he has created can only be the subject of speculation.[2] Jean-Jacques Rousseau was led, through similar reasoning, to the concept of a creator who is necessarily manifest in, as well as to, man, his creature.[3] Lastly, for Diderot, the same starting-point of man's existence led to a theory of the evolution of matter, self-determining and finite.[4]

Mme du Châtelet went along with Voltaire's view some of the way. She agreed with his statements, as, for example, in *Les Lettres philosophiques* that scientific investigation is an activity which is independent of metaphysics and that the *philosophes* should be allowed to pursue scientific enquiry without being accused of seeking to prove or disprove religious and other metaphysical truths. That was the *philosophes*' objective. Mme du Châtelet had a further aim, to bring metaphysical reasoning back in and to apply it to provide the *ratio*, the 'sufficient reason' for the scientists' universe. This novel line, holding a middle ground between empiricism and the acceptance of self-contained metaphysical systems was undoubtedly original.[5]

Following Leibniz, Mme du Châtelet admitted an immaterial level of reality which meant that explanations could transcend the physical, phenomenal level and demonstrate general truths on the borderline of science and metaphysics.[6] As Mme du Châtelet says in her foreword: 'Several truths of physics, meta-

INSTITUTIONS PHYSIQUES

DE *MADAME LA MARQUISE*

DU CHASTELLET

adreſſées à Mr. ſon Fils.

Nouvelle Edition, corrigée & augmentée,
conſiderablement par l'Auteur.

TOME PREMIER.

A **AMSTERDAM,**
AUX DEPENS DE LA COMPAGNIE.
M DCC XLII.

Title page of *Institutions physiques*, vol. 1, Amsterdam, 1742

PRINCIPES
MATHÉMATIQUES

DE LA

PHILOSOPHIE NATURELLE,

Par feue Madame la Marquiſe DU CHASTELLET.

TOME PREMIER.

A PARIS,

Chez { DESAINT & SAILLANT, rue S. Jean de Beauvais,
LAMBERT, Imprimeur - Libraire, rue & à côté
de la Comédie Françoiſe, au Parnaſſe.

M. D. C C L I X.

AVEC APPROBATION ET PRIVILÉGE DU ROI.

Title page of *Principes mathématiques de la philosophie naturelle,*
vol. 1, Paris, 1759

physics and geometry are clearly interlinked.' For this purpose she looked to Leibniz, whose ideas she would explain, having read them in the work of Wolff and having had them explained to her by one of his disciples — she does not name Koenig. She appreciated that experiment was the stick 'given to us by nature to conduct enquiry', but stressed that hypotheses should not be underrated as necessary preliminaries to scientific enquiry (she devoted a whole chapter to the merits of hypotheses, Chapter IV). Most valuable, however, is 'that compass which can guide us in the moving sands of knowledge', Leibniz's principle of sufficient reason. This point is taken up in her first chapter which discusses the principles that must be applied in any pursuit of knowledge.

Knowledge depends upon other knowledge and its acquisition is based on unquestioned principles which must be evident. Mme du Châtelet begins by challenging Descartes' principle of innate ideas, 'a strong, inner sentiment'. When Euclid demonstrated the logic of an equilateral triangle, he did not rely on 'a strong inner sentiment'. Moreover, two philosophical opponents are likely to have two opposite 'strong inner sentiments'. So proofs have to be offered; nothing may be left to the imagination. The first principle, essential in the pursuit of knowledge, requires that contradiction be eliminated, a contradiction being that which both affirms and denies something at the same time. Something cannot be and also not be. This is the basis of certainty.

The term 'impossible' thus applies to that which implies a contradiction; 'possible' to that which does not — and one must be sure when declaring a thing impossible that it is really so because it both affirms and denies something and not because it does not happen to conform to a particular view. This principle is a requirement for every 'necessary' truth, in other words, a truth which can be determined in one way only. For contingent truth, a second principle is required, namely the principle of sufficient reason, which enables one thing to be preferred to another and which makes certainty possible. 'I can assure you that my room is as I left it, being sure that no-one has entered in the meantime. Without the sufficient reason for my statement, I could assure you of nothing'. Or: 'If I can replace some stones by some lead on a scale without affecting the measurement, I can assure you that their weight is identical; I have a sufficient reason for my claim.'

It is important to note here that 'sufficient reason' is both a concept of science, making demonstration possible, and of logic, making intellectual proof possible.

The sufficient reason for the creation of the universe and its structured laws can only be a supreme wisdom; the alternative is that it could only have been caused by chance, that is by nothing.

Nothing can come into being without sufficient reason. The question arises, what is it that determines the selection of that which does come into being? Everything that does not imply a contradiction is possible, but it is not necessarily in being. Everything that does exist must necessarily have been possible; so one can infer possibility from existence, though one cannot infer existence from possibility. Since everything comes into being and then perishes, all things are contingent — and not necessary, for they could also not have come into being. One can look for the sufficient reason for the existence of something either within the thing or outside. But the sufficient reason cannot be within, because, if it were, the thing could not be; it would then not be contingent. So the sufficient reason must be external to the thing.

The sufficient reason cannot be in another contingent thing, nor in a series of contingent things. It can therefore only be in a non-contingent thing, a necessary being, which provides the sufficient reason for the existence of all contingent beings and its own and that being is God. To such a necessary being, Mme du Châtelet now devotes a whole chapter, 'On the existence of God'.

The study of nature leads us up to knowledge of a supreme being. This is a great truth, writes Mme du Châtelet, which is even more important, if that is possible, for good physics than for morality. As already stated, it was important for the *philosophes* to separate morality from theology and from religious associations. Since they saw many of the manifestations of religion as immoral, they gave much thought to possible alternative sources of morality, such as nature or history. A concept of God did not, they believed, offer a guide to human conduct. It was, however, a necessity because without such a concept, the functioning of the universe and of man within it was incomprehensible. Hence the need for such a concept for the scientists, for 'physics'.

Like the *Traité de métaphysique* by Voltaire and the 'Profession de foi du Vicaire savoyard' in *Émile* by Rousseau, Mme du Châtelet's argument begins: I exist; therefore something exists. If something exists, something must always have existed, because nothingness, a negation, could not have produced that which does exist; something cannot exist without having been caused to exist. The being which has existed from all eternity must exist necessarily and not owe his existence to any cause. Mme du Châtelet here presents the deist ontological argument much discussed by her group of friends at Cirey.

Her account continues with the attributes of the supreme being, attributes which follow on the necessity of his existence:

1. He is eternal, that is, has no beginning, since there is nothing which could have brought him into being.
2. He has no end; a necessary being cannot not exist.
3. He is immutable; to exist necessarily must mean existing as he is, neither other nor changing.
4. He must be simple or single, not composite, not such that parts might be dissociated: in other words, whatever there is, is there necessarily once and for all. Matter is different. It is constantly changing and must therefore be contingent. It cannot be the being that exists necessarily. Our soul cannot be the necessary being, since our perceptions are constantly changing.

The being which exists of itself is thus a being different from the world which we see, from matter which makes up the world and from our soul; the sufficient reason for the existence of this being and of all other beings that exist is in this being.

There can only be one necessary being.

As to the world, it is as it is and not otherwise, but there must have been other possibilities; as in novels, events could always have been otherwise. In order to make this world a reality the other possibilities must have been considered, which entails an intellectual activity; so God must be an intelligent being.

Our understanding is effected by a succession of ideas, perceptions, and so on. God's cannot be; he sees everything together clearly, though in a way which we cannot comprehend.

Mme du Châtelet now follows a Leibnizian line of thought: since God chose to realise this world, the creator's choice is the sufficient reason for the existence of this world. Being perfect, God can only have chosen that which was the most perfect, in other words, that in which all the parts tended with the greatest harmony towards an overall purpose. The necessary being is thus infinitely wise since only a being who is infinitely wise can choose that which is most perfect. (The logic is not straightforward here; perfect and wise are given as separate attributes on the basis of the same reason.)

The universe is not a chaos; every part is in its place and could be in no other; things are related, not by a situation but by a design, the imprint of which is everywhere evident; purpose, final causes, are evidence of wisdom. Voltaire would go along with this particular deist argument, though not with the next statement that 'this world is therefore the best of all possible worlds, the one in which the greatest variety is found together with the greatest order, where the greatest number of effects is produced by the simplest laws'.

As for the evils in this world, God suffers them in so far as they are part of the best possible sequence of things; they could not be eliminated without eliminating some perfection in the whole. 'We are not able to know everything, to understand everything, nor to be in every place that would necessitate our presence; *these are faculties which man could not have without becoming God*' (my emphasis). Imperfections are thus necessary 'imperfections'.

The view that if man were perfect, he would not be man but God is one which Voltaire certainly held for most of his life. It figures in the 'Lettre sur Pascal' in the *Lettres philosophiques*, written before Voltaire knew Mme du Châtelet; it still figures as late as 1766 in his *Le Philosophe ignorant*. Mme du Châtelet next reverts to Wolff's reasoning: God cannot make that which is impossible, possible, because things cannot be possible and impossible at the same time. This is not a negation of his omnipotence; it follows on the earlier definition of a contradiction, a necessity both for the rational thinker and the scientist as a premise for making valid statements. It follows that imperfections are included in that set of conditions which make something possible. Of that which is possible, however, God must have chosen the best, given his attribute of wisdom.

Thus, the choice of the best of the possible worlds proves his free will, since he could have chosen any other and brought it into existence and 'to act upon a choice in accordance with one's will is to be free'. Giving reality to the best possible sequence of things, giving as much essential perfection to each part as possible, God shows his infinite goodness; his wisdom guides the unavoidable evils in this sequence of things to a greater good.

God is thus the absolute master of the chain of being. It follows that no contingent creation can persist through any 'force' of its own. Therefore, the reason for continued existence cannot be within creatures which can neither begin nor continue to be, except by the will of the creator whom the creature needs every moment so that it may be sustained in the actual existence which he gave it.

It is clear to any student of Voltaire's work that Mme du Châtelet's exposition assimilates much of the deist thinking adopted by Voltaire into her account of the philosophy of Leibniz. The deist basis appealed to her as it did to contemporary *philosophes*. But she was not satisfied, as they often were, to leave the questions which deism refrains from examining, unanswered. Wolff's exposition of Leibniz satisfied her demand for rational demonstration while allowing her to explore further than would the empiricists. The latter, quite happy to accept God as providing the answer to metaphysical questions, concentrated on the knowable, physical world. Inevitably, this was to lead to a materialist set of answers to all questions. For Mme du Châtelet, neither the Leibnizians nor the Newtonians could be accepted exclusively.

In Chapter VII, Mme du Châtelet undertakes to explain the much discussed monads and to show the difference between the ideas of Leibniz and those of earlier theories which explained matter in terms of atoms (Epicurean) or particles (Gassendi). Leibniz was looking for the sufficient reason for the extension of matter and found it in particles which did not themselves have extension and which he called monads.

Mme du Châtelet was aware of breaking new ground. Most people in France, she wrote, know little more than the term monad, partly because 'the works of the famous Wolff have not been translated into French'. Views which half of Europe accepted, she believed, surely deserved attention. 'I shall therefore try to make you [her son] understand the ideas of these two great philosophers on the origin of matter'.

To say that matter, which has extension, is made up of particles of extended matter is to say nothing, since extended particles of matter are still matter, so that the question remains as before. One needs to look for something non-extended, something without parts and that can only be a simple, non-extended unit. You do not explain a watch in terms of bits of watch, but in terms of wheels and chains which are not 'watch' except in a certain combination.

The will of the creator does not explain extension. It explains actuality — the fact that things come into existence — but not possibility; God chooses to give actuality from among many possibilities. The question that arises is, what is the sufficient reason for the extension of matter, and how can monads provide the answer.

Monads have no parts, no extension, no size or shape, they cannot be seen, touched or represented in any way. If they are to explain composite units, endlessly varied and changing, the simple units, monads, cannot be alike; they must all be dissimilar. To explain change, the sufficient reason requires a principle, a force, and this force must be actual, not only potential; it has to be a continual tendency to activity, impeded only when, for a sufficient reason, it is resisted. And just as the soul of each person produces different ideas, so the internal force of simple, dissimilar units makes for constantly changing, dissimilar things.

To explain durability, simple units must have substance, that is, the property of subsisting; they are true substances in that they have durability and they are susceptible to modification through their internal force. Successive states of simple units must depend on previous ones, only the first depending on God. In the same way a finished clock is the product of a previous stage, itself similarly dependent — only the first arrangement having been determined by the one who conceived it.

All things are interdependent and such interdependence indicates a whole, all the parts of which tend towards one end. The present state of basic elements relates to the present state of the universe as well as to all past and future states. The interdependence expresses harmony in the same way as the proper functioning of a machine requires the harmonised functioning of all its parts. We cannot tell how all things past and future are interrelated, since no finite beings can perceive infinite relationships without being God; yet we are aware that they exist and that is important in itself.

Chapter VII ends somewhat diffidently: 'Truths have always taken years to be accepted. It is not for me to decide whether that applies to the monads of Mr Leibniz. But whether one accepts or refutes them, they cannot diminish the certainty of our research, since we shall never, by our experiments accede to the first elements which constitute physical bodies.'

W. H. Barber[7] shows that while others were also engaged in the task of presenting the German philosophers to the French, Mme du Châtelet's was one of the first accounts of the ideas of Wolff, in particular the chapter on monads; the chapter on the existence of God was based on the ideas of Leibniz.[8] Her book was reviewed in the *Journal des Savants* (March and May 1741) and in the *Mémoires de Trévoux* (Mai 1741). It was clearly regarded as important. Barber quotes one contemporary expert in the field, Deschamps, who writes in his *Cours abrégé de philosophie wolffienne* (1743):

> It is with transports of delight that I have seen an illustrious French woman giving an example to her nation and opening the door to a philosophy which none of them had yet dared to broach and which they regarded as almost indecipherable. They will henceforth no longer be able to tax Wolffianism with obscurity nor with impenetrable depths, since a lady was perfectly capable of understanding it and of explaining it clearly in her own tongue. One cannot assuredly praise Mme du Châtelet too highly and she is entitled to expect the full gratitude not only of Mr Wolff, but equally of the entire world of letters.[9]

Newton's Principia Mathematica, *a translation*

Mme du Châtelet was yet to be considered, with Voltaire, as 'the foremost propagators of Newtonian science in France'.[10] Her contribution was based on the experimental studies set up at Cirey and set out in her own book on Newton, *Principes mathématiques de la philosophie naturelle*[11] which consisted of her translation of Newton's *Principia Mathematica* from Latin and a commentary entitled 'Exposition abrégée du système DU MONDE et explications des principaux Phénomènes astronomiques tirées des Principes de M. Newton'. Not all the commentary was her own work. Much of it was based, as Mme du Châtelet acknowledged, on work undertaken together with the scientist Clairaut; the section on tides was a summary of a prize essay by Daniel Bernoulli. The bulk of the work was hers, namely the first half of the commentary which, the publishers' preface states, enables 'these discoveries which hitherto bristled with so many difficulties to become available to all readers capable of paying some attention and equipped with even a slender acquaintance of mathematics'. Her reputation in the field was evidently well established. 'As to the confidence which the reader may place in this translation', we are told, 'it is enough to say that it is the work of the late Madame la Marquise du Chastellet and that it has been checked by M. Clairaut.' What is more, 'the illustrious interpreter, more jealous of the author's spirit and meaning than of his words has not hesitated to add or transpose ideas in some places in order to give greater clarity to the sense. As a result, Newton will often be found more intelligible in this translation than in the original or even in the English translation.'

Voltaire is, if possible, even more fulsome in his praise. As he wrote in his 'Eulogy': 'We have witnessed two miracles; one, that Newton wrote this work, the other, that a lady has translated and explained it.' Mme du Châtelet's reputation and her sex may have helped the acceptance of Newtonian physics in France. At all events, she established her authority in the field in the eyes of the intelligent reader — one recalls her claim, in the translation of *The Fable of the Bees*, only ever to address herself to the intelligent reader — and her efforts were directed towards making a difficult subject acceptable to that reader. Her success was of significant help in one of the important intellectual battles of the day, fought against a society 'that was almost solidly Cartesian'.[12]

The Newtonian party had Cirey as their foremost camp. Here, with a laboratory and a very well stocked library, Mme du Châtelet and Voltaire invited the experts in the field: Maupertuis, whose *Discours sur les différentes figures des astres* was, in 1732, the first openly Newtonian publication written by a Frenchman;[13] his friend Clairaut, like Maupertuis a member of the Académie des Sciences, whose modification of Newton's classical formulation of gravity as $\frac{a}{x^2}$ to $\frac{a}{x^2} + \frac{a}{mx^4}$[14] was at the centre of a controversy just when Mme du Châtelet was writing her book on Newton; and Count Francesco Algarotti, the young Venetian scientist and poet who read his hosts part of his work in progress, which was addressed to the ladies, *Il Newtonianismo per le dame*. Correspondence with friends and scholars, notably with Frederick of Prussia, spread the debate abroad.

The reluctance of the Cartesian majority to accept the work of Newton was perhaps the reluctance of a rationalist camp to see the powers of reason limited. It is not that Descartes, and for that matter Leibniz, were against the use of experiment; on the contrary. But their reasoning inevitably looked for the metaphysical patterns that would explain observed phenomena. A mechanistic universe would satisfy this. As Fontenelle had put it: 'The claim is that the universe is, on a large scale, what a watch is on a small scale and that everything in it is conducted by regulated movements which depend on the arrangement of the parts'.[15] The 'moderns', the Newtonians, restricted the role of reason to the immediate explanation of observable phenomena, either relegating any design to God or permanently suspending judgement convinced that the possibility of evidence would never become available.

A mechanistic philosophy, where all physical phenomena have mechanistic, that is intelligible causes, was unhappy with inexplicable forces, such as Newton's attraction. Hence a loyalty to Descartes' 'whirls' which, for instance, explained weight as the effect of the centrifugal force of some matter which, circulating around bodies, sweeps them to the centre of its circulation. Attraction as a property of matter appeared highly mysterious, too, as an explanation of motion, where Cartesian theory held to a concept of matter as of itself passive, moved only by an external force. Mme du Châtelet herself was, for many years, unwilling to abandon the metaphysical backing for science. 'One must not', she had written in the *Institutions de physique*, 'allow oneself to be seduced by the ease with which phenomena can be explained by attraction, because there is no effect which cannot easily be explained if one were allowed to imagine causes according to need without taking the trouble of ascertaining whether what one is supposing is contrary to the principle of sufficient reason.'[16]

It is not clear whether Mme du Châtelet was herself finally seduced by Newtonian science; Voltaire, a loyal Newtonian throughout, had been somewhat put out by her apparent defection to the Leibnizians. 'Mme du Châtelet will, no doubt,' he writes to Maupertuis on 29 August 1740, when the *Institutions* was being completed, 'cross your path somewhere. She will arrive together with sufficient reason and surrounded by monads'. In his 'Eulogy', he writes: 'Having made the imaginings of Leibniz intelligible . . . she understood that this metaphysical philosophy, so bold yet with so little basis, did not merit her research . . . She felt that monads and pre-established harmony should be set with Descartes' three elements . . . . Thus, having had the courage to improve Leibniz, she had the courage to abandon him.' An enemy of party-spirit and of systems 'she devoted herself entirely to Newton'.[17]

Voltaire's own knowledge of Newton's work was greatly helped by Mme du Châtelet, if only because her grasp of mathematics was better than his. Ira O. Wade goes further: 'She had a wider outlook on the science of her time and was more open to other, non-Newtonian scientists, more original in her investigations, and more imaginative (but not so very much more) in her approach. The fairest judgement would probably be that Voltaire did more to popularise Newton in France, while she did more to popularise science in general, Newtonian and Leibnizian alike.'[18]

Mandeville's The Fable of the Bees, *a Rendering and a Feminist Manifesto*[19]

The controversy which surrounded Mandeville's work must have been in full swing during Voltaire's stay in England. The debate centred on the third edition (1723) of a satire which had originally appeared as an anonymous pamphlet in 1705, entitled *The Grumbling Hive: or, Knaves Turn'd Honest*. The writer, who had translated a number of fables by La Fontaine and Aesop and had indeed composed several of his own, here presented an entertaining moral tale, in verse, exposing the hypocrisy, greed and cunning of citizens in every walk of life. The somewhat unexpected end showed how, once these people had been converted to honesty, trade, industry and the arts declined; how armies, now above employing mercenaries, were decimated and although

> Their courage and integrity
> At last were crowned with victory

that victory, which left only a minute population alive out of the once mighty, flourishing swarm, was a hollow victory:

They flew into a hollow tree
Blest with content and honesty

— and nothing, the implication is, of substance.

When Mandeville reprinted the poem, it was accompanied by an essay, 'An Enquiry into the Origin of Moral Virtue' and a number of 'Remarks' in prose, short essays each using a phrase or two from the fable as heading. The Remarks grew in number with each subsequent edition. The whole was now entitled *The Fable of the Bees: or, Private Vices, Publick Benefits*, making the point that many vices, in themselves reprehensible, were a necessity to 'the happiest and most flourishing society'. Although Doctor Johnson approved of the work, it was attacked in England in the press, in pulpits and in court — the book was presented as a public nuisance by the Grand Jury of Middlesex. The controversy continued on the continent; in France, it joined the many works condemned to be publicly burnt.[20]

Madame du Châtelet chose to translate *The Fable* not only, as she writes in her translator's preface, as an example of the free, virile thinking of the philosopher nation, but because it is, she believes,

one of the world's works most suited to humanity in general. It is, I believe, the best moral book ever written, that is the one that best enables men to see the true origin of feelings which nearly everyone indulges without examination. The ideas may seem bold . . . but if they teach men to know themselves, the book cannot fail to be useful to thinking people, for whom alone the book is destined.

Mandeville, she claims, deserves to be called the Montaigne of the English — an honour he had already claimed for himself.

Notwithstanding this fulsome praise, Mme du Châtelet thought that Mandeville did not write well and that he sometimes got unduly carried away. 'I have corrected those passages', she writes, 'and cut anything which relates only to the English and their customs'. She has also 'taken the liberty to add reflections' which, not wishing to mislead the reader, she has indicated clearly as additions to the text. These corrections, additions and, indeed, omissions are, of course, highly revealing, as a brief comparison of the texts shows.

The translation of Mandeville's work presented a very personal challenge as well as a technical one. Mme du Châtelet's slight changes of emphasis are indicative of her response. We know from her praise that she approved of Mandeville's book. It is highly probable that the work was the object of study and discussion with Voltaire at Cirey in 1735.[21] Mme du Châtelet did not, in fact, translate *The Fable* itself, partly because it was in verse 'and I don't write any'; partly because, as she says, the ideas were also set out in the 'Remarks', each of which is a short moral treatise independent of *The Fable*. She did not even translate all the 'Remarks', stopping at the twelfth out of Mandeville's twenty-three. Her text thus consists of a translator's preface, the author's preface and introduction — which she runs together and gives as one section — Mandeville's essay 'An Enquiry into the Origin of Moral Virtue' — which forms her Chapter I — and twelve of Mandeville's 'Remarks'.

The value of the translator's preface for the modern reader is not connected with Mandeville; it lies rather in her reflections on the problems of translating and in the passages which give expression to her very determined feminist stance. She explains that not all books lend themselves equally to translation. 'Of all works reasoned ones seem to lend themselves best.' Reason and morality belong to all nations. The individual nature of a language, that curse of all translators, is felt much less in works where ideas only are to be rendered and where beauty of style is not foremost. Works of imagination can rarely be transmitted from one nation to another, since to translate poetry well, one needs to be almost as great a poet oneself. She is aware that translating presents many pitfalls; word for word translations can falsify, a lack of proper understanding of the original can lead to obscurity; worst are those which present the translators' silly ideas instead of the author's. A work on morality, where style does not matter will therefore determine her selection of a suitable text. In England, she adds, one does not need to give so much thought to all this. 'The English do not discriminate . . . the study of French forming part of their education, those able to translate are more numerous amongst them.'

Hers was a very professional approach. After the work by Mandeville, Madame du Châtelet was to tackle the works of

Newton with the same consciousness of the problem. At the same time she had a very period approach to translating. As will be seen, there is little exact rendering of the English text in her version; what we have is rather her rendering of the ideas expressed in the original; and she did not hesitate to cut or change sections which she did not consider of interest to the French reader.

The translator's preface concludes with an apology for having undertaken the task 'seeing that I am a woman'. She evidently writes with great feeling here:

> I feel the full weight of the prejudice which so universally excludes us from the sciences; it is one of the contradictions in life that has always amazed me, seeing that the law allows us to determine the fate of great nations, but that there is no place where we are trained to think. . . . Let the reader ponder why, at no time in the course of so many centuries, a good tragedy, a good poem, a respected tale, a fine painting, a good book on physics has ever been produced by women. Why these creatures whose understanding appears in every way similar to that of men, seem to be stopped by some irresistible force, this side of a barrier. Let people give a reason, but until they do, women will have reason to protest against their education. . . . If I were king . . . I would redress an abuse which cuts back, as it were, one half of human kind. I would have women participate in all human rights, especially those of the mind. It would seem as if they were born only to deceive — this being the only intellectual exercise allowed them. The new education would greatly benefit the human race. Women would be worth more and men would gain something new to emulate. . . . I am convinced that many women are either unaware of their talents by reason of the fault in their education or that they bury them on account of prejudice for want of intellectual courage. My own experience confirms this. Chance made me acquainted with men of letters who extended the hand of friendship to me. . . . I then began to believe that I was a being with a mind. . . .

She ends by saying that she has given great care to her present task: 'Men's injustice in excluding us from the sciences should at least serve to prevent us from writing bad books. Let us try to have this advantage over them, that their tyranny turns into a fortunate necessity for us and that in our works only our names are found fault with.' It is a powerful manifesto that could well have been written by a twentieth-century feminist. It must have seemed progressive indeed to her contemporaries.

Mme du Châtelet then turns to Mandeville's work and translates his preface and introduction. Her rendering of the author's opening statement is a good example of her approach. Mandeville's text reads: 'Laws and Government are to the Political bodies of civil societies what the vital spirits and Life itself are to the natural bodies of animated creatures.' In Mme du Châtelet's translation this becomes the rather more succinct; 'Laws are to society what life is to the human body.' The next few lines are similarly stripped of what may have seemed like wordiness to her. Her changes hint at her views. The English reads:

> they that examine into the nature of man, abstract from art and education, may observe that what renders him a sociable animal, consists not in his desire of company, good nature, pity, affability and other graces of a fair outside; but that his vilest and most hateful qualities are the most necessary accomplishments to fit him for the largest, and according to the world, the happiest and most flourishing societies.

'Abstract from art and education' becomes 'those . . . who, in their research, pay no heed to the prejudices of education'; 'his vilest and most hateful qualities' becomes 'those vices which most gall the preacher'; — there is nothing about 'the happiest and most flourishing society' in her translation.

'Man', the English writer states, 'is a compound of passions governing him in turns; he is not asked. To show that these qualifications are the great support of a flourishing society has been the subject of the poem.' Mme du Châtelet agrees that passions govern us in turns but, for her, as she adds, 'they are the source of our virtues and our vices'. Where the English reader 'may yet by his own imperfections be taught to distinguish virtue and vice', the French reader may, instead, 'be shown how moral good and evil originated'. 'When I say man', adds Mandeville, 'I mean neither Jews nor Christians, but mere men, in the state of nature and ignorance of the true deity.' Mme du Châtelet omits the state of nature and ignorance of the deity. Religion and the deity are not part of her moral analysis.

On a lighter note, too, Mme du Châtelet has the French reader in mind. The English text illustrates the author's thesis of public benefit derived from private vice with the example of the dirty streets of London. Everyone would enjoy clean streets; but if they reflect that all dirt is a result of the bustling trade and the movement of people, 'they will hardly ever wish to see the streets of it less dirty'. Mme du Châtelet simply adds an illustration of her own:

> Society people, rising at midday, are not aware of the labour which the dinner they are being served has cost and how many wagons, animals and people must needs come from the country to the town, to serve them a delicious meal. They see in all this nothing but one of the comforts which has become too ordinary to be worthy of note. But the *philosophe* sees here the industry and labour of a whole people that has worked for his pleasure.

She thus makes a point that has little relevance to the 'public benefit' thesis.

Lastly, in the introduction, one notes the difference between the light-hearted tone of the English author and the serious, utilitarian view of the lady *philosophe*, who cannot think of writing if there is no benefit to society. 'To the question, *cui bono*. . . . Truly, besides the reader's diversion, I believe none at all', writes Mandeville. 'If I were asked', writes the translator, 'why I applied myself to proving all these things, and what advantage men will have from my work, I would reply, naively, that I well feel how difficult it is to correct them and that I fear the truths in it may well not be of use to them.'

Mme du Châtelet makes Mandeville's essay, 'An Enquiry into the Origin of Moral Virtue', which is quite separate from the author's 'Remarks', her first chapter. As before, the translation presents the ideas in the English text in a pithy and succinct form. Mandeville sets out to show by which means law-givers succeeded in getting people to prefer 'the public benefit to private good', given that 'All untaught animals are only solicitous of pleasing themselves, and naturally follow the bent of their own inclinations, without considering the good or harm that from their being pleased will accrue to others'. The law-givers achieved their goal by working on man's natural sensitivity to praise and contempt and his sense of pride, so that, according to Mandeville, 'instructions to the nations in honour and shame led to the first rudiments of morality, rendering men useful to each other as well as tractable'.

Mme du Châtelet inserts a theory of her own. Love and the need to propagate the species was responsible for the origin of society. The need to care for one's own family and the need two families would have of each other, led to a grouping together. The cleverest amongst them realised that man was born with an indomitable pride and the first legislators made this realisation serve to civilise men — a term she likes: where Mandeville speaks of 'how man was broke' she writes 'how man was civilised'. Both agree on the definition of vice and virtue. As the English has it: 'all agreed to call everything which, without regard to the public, man should commit to gratify any of his appetites, VICE. . . . And to give the name of VIRTUE to every performance, by which man, contrary to the impulse of nature, should endeavour the benefit of others, or the conquest of his own passions, out of a rational ambition of being good.' The definition is translated, though the impulse of nature and the conquest of man's own passions is omitted. Again Mme du Châtelet adds a new dimension to the argument. Vice and virtue, she writes, are enshrined in laws or rather, that which the law declares good and bad is what is accepted as virtue and vice; it will vary from country to country, like the rules of games; just as a move may be considered a mistake in one game and be allowed in another, so the terms virtue and vice will fit different acts in Paris and Constantinople. Mme du Châtelet's relativism, which makes morality depend upon climate and conditions is characteristic of the *philosophe* approach, certainly in evidence since Montesquieu's *Lettres persanes* (1721).

Mme du Châtelet, however, does not take the relativist argument the whole way. There is a sense in which morality is universal, she tells us. The content of that which constitutes the well-being of society may vary from place to place, but that still leaves an attitude, a universal rule for all men 'which God himself engraved on their hearts': 'Do not do unto others as you would not have others do unto you.' And surprisingly, this friend of Voltaire accuses Locke, the English philosopher, of having gone too far when he rejected notions of universal morality. All societies, she counters, expect promises to be kept, an example Mandeville also uses elsewhere. The divine injunction, she believes, accords with a natural feeling of benevolence for our species — another idea currently under discussion by the *philosophes* — and is as involuntary as hunger or thirst. There would thus seem to be two natural impulses, benevolence for the species and love of self. The latter is stronger and, whenever our self-interest is involved, this will stifle the benevolence. Laws and punishments, writes Mme du Châtelet, prevent our self-interest from winning over the dictates of nature (the benevolence). This interesting formulation which sees benevolence as natural, almost cancels out Mandeville's hypothesis that politicians and legislators curb a 'natural' self-interest and instil an 'artificial' concern for the well-being of society, 'public benefit'. Mme du Châtelet is not being inconsistent; one remembers her earlier intercalation which had stated that society originated with love and procreation. The French reader needed to be fully alert to quotation marks at the beginning and end of Mme du Châtelet's additions in order not to be confused as to the ideas of the original.

The next section of the essay presents no problems to the translator, expressing as it does the argument, so often voiced by the *philosophes*, that morality does not originate in religion. Mandeville explains that idol worship and superstition in Egypt, Greece and Rome did not prevent those nations from having elaborate codes of morality.

The English essay concludes by saying that if the reader thinks that these ideas on the origin of moral virtue are 'offensive to Christianity', he should consider that there is no better evidence of divine wisdom than 'that MAN whom Providence has designed for Society' should 'receive from a seeming necessity of natural causes, a tincture of that knowledge in which he was afterwards to be made perfect by the true religion, to his eternal welfare'. This apparent deference to religious authority may well be a formality. Mme du Châtelet's pithy rendering is more neutral:

If some readers condemn these ideas on the origin of moral virtue and think they are offensive to Christianity, I hope that they will see how unjustified such a suspicion is when they consider that nothing can better justify the impenetrable depths of providence than to show that the weakness of man, whom it created for society, can serve his happiness and that of others.

This is rather different from Mandeville's thinking; it certainly shows no concern for 'true religion'. Ira Wade has shown[22] that there is a clear relationship between *The Fable* and Voltaire's *Traité de métaphysique*, Chapters VIII and IX. Referring to Mme du Châtelet's additions, Wade shows that they figure in the *Traité*, often in strikingly similar formulations.[23] He instances her formulation 'There is a universal law for all men, which God himself has engraved on their hearts'. This appears in the Voltaire text as 'It seems clear to me that there are natural laws which men throughout the world must agree, even against their will'. The reader may find a difference between the two formulations; it is very much the same kind of difference that is apparent between Mandeville's text and Mme du Châtelet's 'translation'.

The main body of Mandeville's book, the 'Remarks', elicits few comments from the translator. The first few chapters are left more or less as they are in the original; they show how traders and businessmen make a living through the needs and vices of others and that such notions as honour and modesty arise with sociability — there is no immodesty when one is alone.

Remark E, touching on one of Mme du Châtelet's own passions, gambling, does elicit a response. She enters into the psychology of the gambler who never reveals the extent of his losses and tells the reader that as half the life of society people is spent gambling, to observe this is useful to the *philosophes*, the only people who study their fellow men carefully and are able to discern the different passions beneath the countless forms that these assume. Gambling also allows men of the world to show their humanity:

> If a poor man dies of hunger in the street or a coachman perishes of cold waiting for his master the whole night, they cannot feel for them, since they have never had a similar experience nor do they expect to have. But, having frequently experienced misfortune when playing and fearing constantly that their luck may well turn, they have a regard for those from whom they are winning money which, they hope will be accorded to them when they lose

This illustration may also exemplify her earlier justification of the universal law 'Do not do unto others as you would not have others do unto you'.

Some chapters are considerably shorter than the original, for instance, Remark G which shows how the wicked, especially innkeepers, can yet serve society. Remark H shows that opposites need one another in society: virtuous women and priests need the presence of prostitutes in order to keep husbands content and honourable, so that 'chastity may be supported by incontinence and the best virtues want the assistance of the worst vices'. Mme du Châtelet may well have approved the more serious opening paragraph of this Remark which describes the advantages of being a religious opposition: 'Nothing was more instrumental in forwarding the Reformation than the sloth and stupidity of the Roman clergy; yet the same Reformation has roused them from the laziness and ignorance they then laboured under.' So, too, other clerics, as also in England, by reproaching their opponents for their ignorance have spurred the latter into becoming a learned and formidable opposition. Where there is no opposition, as in Spain and Italy, the clergy is debauched and ignorant.

Mme du Châtelet's text stops with Remark L, on luxury — again a much discussed topic of the day. It is possible that she wearied of the task. For the twelve pages of the original her text gives just over one and, of that, one paragraph is her addition. Her comment underlines a point only implied in the English. 'What is termed luxury', she writes, 'varies with time, country and usage.' 'In Spain, if one wishes to describe a house which lacks nothing, one says: and what is more, it has glass windows.' The modern reader of Voltaire inevitably thinks of the castle of Thunder-ten-tronkh, in *Candide*, the best of all possible castles because 'it has doors and windows'.

The last sentence of Mandeville that is translated reads in English: 'People may go to Church together, and be all of one mind as much as they please, I am apt to believe that when they pray for their daily bread, the bishop includes several things in that petition which the sexton does not think on.' For once, the French version is almost more picturesque: 'A town goes to Church together, but when they pray for their daily bread, the bishop who recites the *pater noster*, the gentleman, the bourgeois and the clerk each understands the words differently.'

Three Chapters of a Grammaire raisonnée

A keenly interested student of mathematics and philosophy might not, nowadays, be expected to write about grammar. The eighteenth-century reader would not have found this so strange; the rational scrutiny of every aspect of life was one of the aims of the *philosophes*. Voltaire's interest in language is well known and it was clearly shared by Mme du Châtelet. 'The study of language was one of her main preoccupations', wrote Voltaire, adding with evident approval that in the midst of the uncertainties and peculiarities of grammar, she displayed 'that spirit of philosophy which should everywhere rule and be the guiding thread in every labyrinth'.[24]

Mme du Châtelet's *Grammaire* was not published by her and we do not know whether it was ever a completed text. All we have are three chapters, found among the Voltaire papers in Leningrad and published by Ira O. Wade.[25] The dating of the *Grammaire* is uncertain; the only piece of internal evidence, an example taken from Voltaire's *L'Enfant prodigue* presented in October 1736, indicates only that the text was written after this date.[26]

Although they did not break any really new ground, theories of language were much discussed and written about in the first half of the eighteenth century. They were frequently influenced by a seventeenth-century work, *La Grammaire de Port-Royal* or *Grammaire raisonnée*, as it was referred to, by Antoine Arnauld and Claude Lancelot,[27] a work which demonstrated the logical relation between reason and language.[28] Mme du Châtelet makes a number of references to this earlier *Grammaire raisonnée*.

Languages, writes Mme du Châtelet, in the first of the extant chapters, Chapter VI, are based on a natural logic which everyone possesses. The specifically *philosophe* ingredient in this assertion is the term 'natural', which links it to the conviction that there are natural — as distinct from man-made or divinely revealed — codes by which man lives, that there exists a natural law and a natural religion and that research into these will discover the best guide for man. This natural logic, she writes, has rules; we cannot ascertain these clearly from observation, but we are helped by the knowledge that the mind operates in the same way in all climates, in other words in all men, and the rules, therefore, will be much the same in all nations. If we wish to understand the rules of language, we must understand logic.

Speech is used to express 'operations of the soul on the objects of our ideas'. This somewhat clumsy description separates ideas from that which ideas perceive, namely 'objects', and from thought processes, namely 'operations of the soul'. One might have expected the word 'mind' rather than 'soul'. In the context of the next few passages, the two terms are used without differentiation. The mind thus holds ideas and directs them at objects, that is, applies them by means of certain mental processes. The description of how language represents what is going on in the mind is what Mme du Châtelet terms grammar.

The 'operations' are next subdivided into three functions: perceiving, judging and reasoning. Judgement is always involved in speech; even simple perceptions cannot be expressed without making a judgement. When I say 'I see a man', I am expressing the judgement that the object I see has an assemblage of features to which I usually give the name 'man'. A judgement has three necessary components, each of which is expressed by a different category of word. A judgement must have a subject and an attribute as well as a kind of word which will link or separate the subject and attribute. To formulate a judgement is to affirm or to deny something and that is why all three kinds of word are required. They may not always be present, but they are always subsumed in our statements.

The words which represent the mental operation form one category of words and those which represent the objects or our perceptions constitute another category. In Chapters VII and VIII Mme du Châtelet describes the two categories of words. The words which represent the objects of our perceptions can be divided into nouns, articles, comparatives, pronouns, prepositions and adverbs; she describes the function and usage of each in turn. She begins in a rather philosophical vein, discussing the metaphysical basis of what she is describing. 'Everything is grounded in metaphysics and especially grammar', she writes.

Mme du Châtelet sees substantives as designating an assemblage of permanent properties while adjectives designate variable properties, 'that is their true metaphysical meaning'. Substance, in metaphysics, she continues, is that which subsists of itself and grammar has taken over this definition for nouns. In grammar, the term 'substantive' designates words which subsist of themselves, whether the assemblage of properties they denote is permanent or variable. Thus 'red', adjective and variable, can become substantive, as in the sentence 'red tires the eye'.

Looking at the other category, Mme du Châtelet begins by noting that while both subject and attribute represent objects of our perception, the words which join the attribute to the subject express an activity of the mind; they express the manner of perceiving the objects. For instance, in the proposition 'this paper is white', the word 'is', which joins the attribute to the subject, expresses an activity of the mind, the activity being an affirmation, since the word 'is' signifies nothing other than that I affirm the whiteness of the paper. A verb is thus a word by means of which one affirms the attribute of a subject. One might think that one verb only, namely 'to be' would be needed for the purpose of affirming. But, since the verb 'to be' always requires the presence of an attribute that is to be affirmed and since people are always seeking to shorten speech, it was possible to reduce the formulation of judgements from three words to two. 'Plato is writing' became 'Plato writes', which explains the origin of the multitude of verbs in every language.

The statement that the essential and proper function of the verb is to affirm is in line with *La Grammaire de Port-Royal*. On more than one occasion, however, Mme du Châtelet does not hesitate to take issue with the authors of that work. She does not accept, for instance, that French has no cases, no imperative or optative, just because there are no grammatical inflections or special forms signifying these. She argues that the French language can and does express them, though perhaps not as clearly as Latin, by such means as prepositions and word order.

Mme du Châtelet appears to be less interested to examine how certain rules of language express certain mental processes than to examine the relationship between the two. The relationship is frequently rationalised. She notes that languages do not have an imperative of the verbs 'to want' and 'to be able'. That is because one cannot order someone 'to be able' or 'to want'. For we are masters neither of our will nor of our ability — 'that is why one asks God to let us want or be able'. True, Spanish is an exception and does have an imperative of 'to want', 'apparently to indicate to men that if they were to make greater efforts, they might frequently do that which appears to be impossible'. The rationalising is evident, but it is a usage and not a grammatical rule that is rationalised. Here, once again, Mme du Châtelet has a modern, scientific approach and looks to evidence. Usage provides the evidence and is to be distinguished from illustrations which are adduced to bear out rules.

As she writes in her last paragraph, the many exceptions and variations in language cannot be reduced to principles and are accepted on the basis of usage alone. Because such peculiarities of language exist, the most skilled grammarian will always make some mistakes when speaking, if he does not master usage, and a person living in the best society, one which uses the finest language, will yet commit countless grammatical errors in writing if his knowledge of the rules derives from usage alone. 'Therefore, to write correctly and with elegance, the rules of grammar must combine with the usage practised by people who speak with elegance.'[29] Mme du Châtelet is clearly an observant student of language and not a dogmatist.

Examen de la Genèse, the Bible Commentary of a Philosophe

In his *Correspondence littéraire*, Grimm relates that Mme du Châtelet and Voltaire had a session every morning when they would read and discuss a chapter or so of the Bible. Apparently, both would make notes and each later used the material for a work on the Scriptures.[30] Voltaire used some of the material in his *La Bible enfin expliquée*, which was not published until 1766, and it is assumed that Mme du Châtelet's version is the *Examen de la Genèse*, a commentary on the Pentateuch and on the New Testament. Her work, however, was not published and a manuscript copy is extant in the municipal library at Troyes.[31] Similarities in expression and outlook between this work and several works of biblical criticism by Voltaire have been discussed by Ira O. Wade.[32] Mme du Châtelet's text was also in line with a large number of clandestine manuscripts, copied and distributed in France at the time, works of critical deism, frequently derived from Spinoza's *Tractatus theologico-politicus* (1670). These texts discussed such things as miracles, prophecies and the morality of the Scriptures. As Wade writes: 'Since these special features had been presented as proofs of the divinity of Christianity, these clandestine writers submit them to a rigorous examination, by testing the accuracy and credibility of the facts as they are related in the Scriptures.'[33] That is exactly what Mme du Châtelet does in her *Examen de la Genèse*. Her work was written over a number of years, the early parts belonging to the period 1737–42. It is a running commentary on the biblical text, in which she examines each episode, picking out verses or sections, which she quotes in Latin, then usually translates and discusses. A rapid look at her commentary on Genesis which, scholars agree, is clearly her work — there are doubts as to some of the later sections — will give a good indication of her approach and method.

In the introduction, Mme du Châtelet sets the tone. God is too human, his relationship to the Jews is not logical, the language is too obscure:

> In Genesis, Moses depicts God as a labourer who does his work, bit by bit, who takes six days to make heaven and earth and who rests on the seventh as if he were tired from too great an achievement that week. It [Genesis] presents him as capable of jealousy, anger, vengeance and repentance, in short with all the defects of man.
>
> If God had wanted to depict himself in a comprehensible way, he should at least have depicted himself with those qualities which make men respected and not with those which cause them to be hated or despised. And let it not be said that it was to relate to the crudeness of the Jews that God did this because, first of all, God did not intend this book for the Jews alone, since it is still today the basis of the religion which his son brought to mankind and he did not rectify our ideas on creation; secondly, the cruder the Jews were, the less reason is there to present the divinity to them in degrading images; they would be incapable of rising above these. But the answer, that God's presentation of himself was in conformity with the crudeness of the Jews, contains another absurdity; because most of the books of the Old Testament are impenetrably obscure and that is so in matters which it was most important for the Jews to know. If a redemption is foretold, if ills are predicted with which God will in the end punish their so-called hard-heartedness, this is done in the form of allegories and figures which the most subtle minds cannot penetrate, let alone a crude people. Yet it mattered much more that they should be

spoken to intelligibly when it was a question of their avoiding total destruction and of benefiting from the redeemer God was to send them, than when they were being told how God set about creating heaven and earth. So the pretension that God supposedly related the crude ideas we have of him in the Old Testament to the crude character of the Jews cannot excuse the manner in which the Supreme Being is being spoken of.

Mme du Châtelet's dissatisfaction emerges clearly and she does not hesitate to offer advice on what the Scriptures should have presented. She takes every account of crude behaviour at face value, and questions the ways of God and the sequence of events as presented by 'Moses or the one who wrote Genesis'.

A rational, scientific point of view is the implied basis for her comments. Unfortunately, the biblical narrative does not lend itself to either rational or scientific analysis. Contradictions arise frequently from the sequence of events in the text. The first two chapters are already full of these. How can the text say 'and there was not a man to till the ground' (II,5), when man had already been created (I,27). How amusing to have the first three days marked off by a morning and evening, before the sun was created on the fourth day. Mme du Châtelet clearly enjoys picking out such examples. When Joseph dreams that the sun, the moon and eleven stars bow down to him, how can Jacob say, 'Shall I and thy mother and thy brothers indeed come to bow down to thee' (XXXVII, 10), when Rachel, his mother, had died two chapters earlier.

Science, she believes, provides many arguments against the text.

Every discovery in physics and astronomy shows up a new absurdity in the story of the creation. For instance, God makes no other difference between the sun and the moon than that he calls the one *the greater light* and the other *the lesser light*, yet children now know that the moon is an opaque body which frequently does not rule the night and which never gives any light other than that of the sun which is reflected towards us

and she wonders how God can divide the light from the darkness, as if darkness were a thing which can be separated from light; darkness cannot be mingled with light in the first place, since it is nothing but the deprivation of light. She wonders, too, how the dove could have brought back a green olive leaf to Noah — it could hardly have been green under the water, since most plants would have died. The text, of course, does not say green but 'fresh'. That does not worry her. For a scientist, Mme du Châtelet is rather often careless in her reading of the text. She is surprised that Jacob, making peace with Laban, should swear 'by the God of Abraham and the God of Nahor' (XXXI, 53) when Nahor, Laban's father, was an idol worshipper. How can Jacob swear by the God of an idol-worshipper? In the biblical text, it is in fact Laban who uses this formula; Jacob swears 'by the fear of Isaac', his own father.

She is convinced of the barbarism of the Jews of the Bible. Circumcision, which worried many *philosophes*, was an example of this. She is amazed that all those who do not obey the commandment to be circumcised should, according to her reading, be punished by death 'which is just like damning all children who die without baptism'. In the actual text, the punishment is that such a one 'shall be cut off from his people'(XVII, 14), a severe punishment indeed, but hardly death. She is particularly revolted by the story of the action taken to avenge Dinah, the daughter of Jacob. The text reads: 'And Shechem . . . the Prince of the land, saw her [Dinah]; and he took her and lay with her and humbled her . . . and Shechem loved the damsel. And Shechem spoke to his father Hamor, saying "Get me this damsel to wife" ' (XXXIV, 2–4). Mme du Châtelet's version has much less justification for acts of vengeance: 'The son of the king of Shechem had fallen in love with Dinah, the daughter of Jacob and had carried her off to make her his wife.' And Mme du Châtelet, who is so upset by the concept of a vengeful God, is here amazed that the descendants of Levi, one of the two brothers responsible for the act of vengeance, could later have been chosen for the temple service — she would, it seems, hold the descendants guilty for ever after.

Almost always Mme du Châtelet sympathises with anyone who suffers at the hand of the patriarchs, as she calls Abraham and all his descendants. How kind the Canaanites must have been, in her view, that a young lad like Joseph could be sent alone through the fields to look for his brothers; how generous a people they must have been to offer Abraham the cave in which he wished to bury his wife, Sarah, as a present. Laban, too was a really friendly person, reproaching Jacob for leaving him without telling him, so that he, Laban, was deprived of the pleasure of accompanying Jacob 'with mirth, with songs, with tabret and with harp' (XXXI, 27). Esau was, at heart, 'the kindest man in the world', she writes, never trying to pay back Jacob's trickery. And as for Pharaoh, he must have been out of his mind to hand the government of Egypt to Joseph just because he had interpreted a dream, and this even before anyone could tell whether the interpretation was valid.

The treatment of animals as equal to men in Genesis amazes Mme du Châtelet. In what language did the serpent speak to Eve? Did God give the serpent reason and speech, specifically to tempt man? And God treats animals just as he treats people. 'Be fruitful and multiply' is said to both man and animals and God makes a covenant with men and with animals after the flood. In Egypt, the first born of men and of animals die in the last of the ten plagues. It is commanded that animals rest on the seventh day and, if an ox has gored a man or woman, it is to be stoned, not the owner. Man is seen simply as *primus inter pares*, so that when animals die, as in the flood, it appears as unjust in her eyes as the revenge upon the people of Shechem.

Mme du Châtelet takes a very independent line on events and on God's doings. Why did God need to go and find out how many righteous men there were in Sodom; did he not know? Why did Lot offer virgins to the Sodomites — they would hardly want them! Why did God not give a warning of the flood, to allow the people to repent, and why drown the animals? And she is most indignant that the burden of original sin on all mankind should be the consequence of Adam's disobedience. Why did God wait to send a redeemer; if he had been sent then, it may not have been necessary to drown everybody. She is unhappy that things are sometimes to be taken literally and not at other times. On the one hand, why should the blessing Isaac spoke to Jacob but intended for Esau, stay with Jacob just because that was how it came out? On the other, why spend a great deal of time on the blessing Jacob gave to Judah, 'the famous prophecy, which has been twisted in so many ways to make it apply to the Messiah'. The Authorised Version has:

The sceptre shall not depart from Judah
Nor the ruler's staff from between his feet
As long as men come to Shiloh;
And unto him shall the obedience of the peoples be.

(XLIX, 10)

The Latin she quotes is rather different: '*Non auferetur sceptrum de Juda et Dux de femore ejus, donec veniat qui mittendus est, et ipse erit expectatio gentium*', which Mme du Châtelet translates as: 'The sceptre will not be taken away from Judah and there will always be a leader from his loins until the one who is to be sent has come and he will be the one expected by the nations.' The Hebrew, she writes, has *donec veniat Silho* and people do not know the meaning of the word 'Silho'. Dom Calmet, her favourite commentator who, incidentally, was also a friend,[34] suggests *donec veniat finis ejus* (until his (Judah's) end has come). If 'Silho' refers to the Messiah and supposing Jesus was that Messiah, how accurate is this prophecy, she asks. Saul, the first king, did not belong to the tribe of Judah: the high priests who ruled for a time were Levites, as were the Maccabees. So the sceptre was no longer with Judah. When Jesus was born, Herod, the ruler, was not even a Jew; nor was the sceptre with Judah either during or after the Babylonian captivity. Any one of these would suffice to show that the prophecy was false and that the meaning which Christianity forced onto Jacob's pronouncement has not come true, she concludes.

Nor did Moses 'or the one who wrote Genesis' know about the unity of God. Here too, she relies on the comments of Dom Calmet: his *Commentaire littéral* and *Dictionnaire de la Bible* were used both by Mme du Châtelet and by Voltaire.[35] Her evidence is that the text of Genesis uses the plural form (*Elohim*) to denote God, as, for example, in the statement 'God created'. The Latin text has the singular *Deus creavit*. But Dom Calmet suggests that the Hebrew intended a plural. Likewise, Adam is driven from the Garden of Eden 'lest he become like one of *us*'. And when the Tower of Babel was built, God said, 'Come, let *us* go down and there confound their language' (XI, 5). It's just as well, she concludes, that the Trinity could resolve the difficulty.

Sceptical as she so often is, Mme du Châtelet accepts things occasionally without question. 'It is historically proven', she writes, 'that no coins were in use before the time of Darius'. Since

Abraham pays coins for the cave he buys and since we are told that Joseph was sold by his brothers for twenty pieces of silver, 'this is undubitable proof that the Pentateuch was written after the time of Moses'. Nor does she hesitate to declare other 'proofs'. The sons of Jacob, she writes, must have been idol-worshippers because Jacob tells his household and all that were with him 'put away the strange gods that are among you' (XXXV, 2). Joseph, too, she is convinced, must have worshipped other gods, the gods of Egypt, the proof being that, as an Egyptian, he ate separately from the Hebrews; we know that the Egyptians did not eat with the Hebrews, she writes, and gives the reference (XLIII, 32) which reads: 'And they set on for him by himself and for them by themselves and for the Egyptians that did eat with him by themselves; because the Egyptians might not eat bread with the Hebrews'. There were three sets of food, in fact, one for the ruler, Joseph, one for the Hebrews and one for the Egyptians.

Mme du Châtelet's scepticism is occasionally expressed in the form of sarcasm. 'No one can fail to see that the statement "the woman shall bruise the serpent's head" means that God will send his only son on earth to hang; it is self-evident'. Other formulations echo the style of Voltaire, as when the angel with whom Jacob struggles asks his name and tells him that it will henceforth be Israel; Jacob then asks the angel his name (XXXII, 29) 'doubtless wanting to change the other's name also'. As to the identity of that angel 'some say it was the second person of the Trinity, others say it was the devil — a fine alternative'.

Altogether, Mme du Châtelet, the *philosophe*, cannot accept either what is said and done in Genesis or what is not said and done. She cannot take the Church Fathers' 'usual excuse that God had commanded it'. Nor can she accept St Augustine's statement, which she quotes as a comment on the many apparent inconsistencies: 'The authority of this book is greater than the capacity of man's mind.' Her comments show very clearly her rejection of a specific concept of God. In her *Institutions de physique* the limitations of man's understanding of the universe and its laws were comfortably acceptable and reflected a trusting conviction that that was how God had arranged it; she had satisfied herself that she had demonstrated the existence of such a God on a rational foundation. The physical world she examined there does not contradict the deity she has posited. In Genesis, the features of God that she reads into the text are much too human to match her 'scientific' concept of God.

Discours sur le bonheur, *a Personal View*

The *Discours sur le bonheur* was published posthumously in 1779. R. Mauzi in the preface to his scholarly edition of the text (1961) suggests that it was probably written between May, 1746 and April, 1748, at about the same time as Diderot's *Pensées philosophiques* and just before Voltaire's tale of a quest for happiness, *Zadig*. While writing the *Discours*, Mme du Châtelet was also hard at work on her translation of Newton's *Principia Mathematica*.

The philosophical quest for happiness was seen by many contemporaries as a great innovation, the glorious discovery of the period, writes Mauzi,[36] and he lists more than a dozen works on the subject of the time. Mme du Châtelet was thus no great innovator. The merit of her short treatise lies in a rather personal response to the subject which is yet conditioned by contemporary ideas. The *Discours* echoes a number of major themes of the period just ending, as, for instance, the Epicurean cult of enjoyment, and voices ideas just emerging, such as the notion of conscience as the arbiter of morality. To these Mme du Châtelet adds her personal plea for a place for passion and illusion.

The readership is clearly specified: 'I am writing for people known as "les gens du monde" (men of the world)', people who are 'born with a ready-made fortune' such that it allows them to live in accordance with their station without shame. This may seem to us to express a rather snobbish point of view. Her readers, however, would have found it quite natural. It was to them, the 'men of the world' that she offered her recipe: 'To be happy, one must rid oneself of prejudice, be virtuous, healthy, have a capacity for enjoyment and for passion and the ability to lend oneself to illusion.' Much of this represents a typical eighteenth-century attitude; to expose prejudice as unworthy of a rational citizen was one of the objects of the *philosophes*' battles; to be virtuous was no new ideal, either, though to link virtue and health was only to become fashionable a few years later, when Jean-Jacques Rousseau would draw attention to the Spartan model and denounce his contemporary society for its greedy and corrupt lifestyle.[37] Enjoyment, in this case 'le goût', an appreciation of quality, was esteemed by many, in particular by those who let the head rule the heart. It is more surprising to find that the experience of passion also matters — that was not at all part of the programme. It did not become significant as an ingredient of fulfilment until the nineteenth century, when the Romantics were to measure superiority by force of emotion. Lastly, illusion, again a fairly unexpected ingredient. Writers in the 1730s, notably Marivaux, were fascinated by the role illusion played in human relationships and later in the century Rousseau was to show how illusion could be a source of aesthetic pleasure and of happiness. In the *Discours*, the concept is not particularly sophisticated. Illusion, necessarily misleading, might be thought to be harmful, but it is not, we are told. While it does not show objects exactly as they are, it adapts them to our nature, so that we may have pleasurable sensations. Just as in optics, where we are not deceived when we see things not as they really are, 'they are shown to us in the way it is useful to us to see them'. We laugh at puppets and at a comedy only if we can lend ourselves to the illusion — we know that the characters are dead while we watch them living and speaking in alexandrine verse. 'Like passions,' she writes, 'illusion is not something you can have if it is not in your nature. However, you can avoid looking behind the scenes.' Most of our pleasures are derived from illusions, she adds, which may be just a wistful reflection or a profound aesthetic observation.

The ambivalence between head and heart appears throughout the *Discours*. On the one hand Mme du Châtelet declares, as any salon lady might, that our sole aim in life is to procure agreeable sensations and sentiments for ourselves — avoid having regrets, do not dwell on your mistakes or on anything unpleasant such as death. On the other, she enjoins the reader not to heed the moralists who preach self-control. They are people who, having no capacity for passion, must needs be satisfied with 'des goûts'. While it is true that passions cause suffering — and these are the only ones playwrights find of interest — there is no happiness without passion. Mauzi has shown[38] that the meaning of the word 'passion' was at this time in the process of changing from a term denoting any emotion, as, for example, fear or hope, to its modern sense of a specific and exclusive emotion, overpowering and concentrated on a single object. Mme du Châtelet uses the word mainly in the modern sense, conscious as she is of her own passionate temperament. And yet, the earlier, wider meaning is still there and with it that same notion of self-control of which she has just been accusing the moralists. Passions, for her, are not of value in themselves and should be indulged only in so far as they lead to happiness. This being the goal, 'there is no passion we cannot overcome once we are truly convinced that it can lead only to unhappiness'. Her examples are highly personal. Suppose you have a passion for food, should you indulge in it — remembering that to be healthy is also a necessary part of the recipe for happiness. Yes, she writes, you should; just use your skill so that it does you no harm. If I am greedy, she tells the reader, I make up for it by dieting. And anyway, when I have overdone things, food does not appeal to me, so then I can make myself healthy again without feeling deprived. What is more, *'la gourmandise'* has the advantage that it may be enjoyed in old age. So can another, more questionable passion, gambling. Mme du Châtelet, as we know, lost considerable sums at the card-table. She suggests that it is well to be moderate here and to reserve this passion for old age when it may become a necessity, there being few others available then. Gambling, she tells us, corresponds to our innate need to be moved by hope or fear; and this is valuable, because happiness depends on having the wherewithal to attain the fullest consciousness of our existence — a highly modern view. And this, gambling offers us. It keeps us in an emotional state and thus taps one of the major sources of happiness we have.

One passion in which Mme du Châtelet indulged and which she strongly recommends for women in particular is studying. Women need the love of study 'to console them for everything which makes them dependent upon men' and to let one's happiness depend on others is to put it at risk. With study she associates another passion, one from which 'no superior being is ever totally exempt', fame — her term is the untranslatable *'gloire'*. Fame may itself be an illusion, she concedes, although the feeling of pleasure which it affords is not illusory. Men, she writes, do not need the passion of study to acquire *gloire*. It is certain that Mme du Châtelet's own pursuit of knowledge was carried out with passionate enthusiasm. It is also well known that she gloried in her reputation as a scholar — especially since it did not require her to abandon jewellery and pompoms.

Mme du Châtelet does not, of course, omit the passion of love from her list. Every faculty in our being, she writes, should be made to sense love and 'once it is lost, one should stop living'. But she is realistic and, aware that illness and frailty have irrevocably lost her the passion of the man 'who subjugated my soul', she accepts that she can be fairly happy with the rather calmer feeling of friendship and her passion for studying.

Mme du Châtelet shared the eighteenth-century approval of *sensibilité*. A superior person is distinguished by the ability to respond emotionally, to be moved. Stimuli will depend on personality, in her case a piece of porcelain or a new piece of furniture will be sufficient. And that is because she does not have a great many of them — not quite true, if we remember the description of her bathroom! Kings, who have a surfeit of fine things, need to find happiness elsewhere, for instance in making their subjects happy. Once more the *philosophe* in her has surfaced. Or perhaps she had in mind the hopes she once had that the *philosophe* Prince Frederick of Prussia, when king, would devote himself to promoting the happiness of his people.

The well-being of society was a key idea in the political thinking of the time. If a king succeeds here, writes Mme du Châtelet, his state will be 'foremost in happiness as in strength'. Virtue, for her, was a social value; it was an essential ingredient in her recipe for happiness, and she defines it as 'everything which contributes to the happiness of society and consequently to our happiness as members of society'. Now, just as the reader is impressed by her 'modern' view, he is taken aback by a conventional statement that one such virtue is '*les bienséances*', doing what is socially correct. These express time-honoured truths, she maintains, and that is reason enough to prevent any decent person from deviating in the slightest from what is agreed as seemly. A sin against the mores of society is a vice; and vice and happiness are incompatible — a thought Mme du Châtelet shared with Rousseau and with many contemporary deists. An approving conscience offers an inner contentment, necessary for the soul's health. Once again, the enlightened view which makes conscience the arbiter of morality is accompanied by the period view that those who sin against virtue, in this sense, will suffer not only the disapproval of their conscience but a sentence far worse than any criminal sentence, public opprobrium (*mépris*). This does not apply to thieves and murderers, she hastens to add, but then 'they are not to be found in the class of those for whom I am writing'.

Notes

1. Letter of 11 August 1740.
2. Voltaire, *Traité de métaphysique*.
3. J. J. Rousseau, *Émile*, 'Profession de foi du vicaire savoyard'.
4. Diderot, *Le Rêve de d'Alembert*.
5. Cf. Linda Gardiner Janik, 'Searching for the metaphysics of science: the structure and composition of Mme du Châtelet's *Institutions de physique*, 1737–40', in *Studies on Voltaire and the Eighteenth Century*, vol. 201, pp. 85–113.
6. Ibid., p. 107.
7. W. H. Barber, *Leibniz in France*, p. 128ff.
8. Ibid., p. 139.
9. Ibid., p. 140.
10. Ira O. Wade, *The Intellectual Development of Voltaire*, p. 445.
11. Published posthumously, the title page bears the date 1759; the Royal privilege was granted in 1746. Cf. I. B. Cohen, 'The French translation of Isaac Newton's *Philosophiae Naturalis Principia Mathematica*' in *Archives Internationales d'Histoire des Sciences*, nos 84–5.
12. Wade, *The Intellectual Development of Voltaire*, p. 473.
13. J. Roger, *Les Sciences de la vie dans la pensée française au XVIIIème siècle*, p. 469.
14. Ibid., p. 483.
15. Fontenelle, *Entretiens sur la pluralite des mondes*, premier soir.
16. *Institutions de physique*, p. 346.
17. Voltaire, 'Eloge', see Appendix.
18. Cf. Wade, *The Intellectual Development of Voltaire*, p. 445.
19. Published in I.O. Wade, *Studies on Voltaire with some unpublished papers by Madame du Châtelet*.
20. Cf. B. Mandeville, *The Fable of the Bees*, (ed.) P. Harth, introduction.
21. Wade, *The Intellectual Development of Voltaire*, p. 347.
22. Cf. Wade, *Studies on Voltaire*, p. 68ff., 'The presentation of the *Traité* to Mme du Châtelet'.
23. Ibid., pp. 70–3.
24. Voltaire, 'Eulogy', see Appendix.
25. Wade, *Studies on Voltaire*, pp. 209–41.
26. Ibid., p. 127.

27. *Grammaire générale et raisonnée contenant les fondements de l'art de parler, expliqués d'une manière claire et naturelle, les raisons de ce qui est commun à toutes les langues et des principales différences qui s'y rencontrent, et plusieurs remarques nouvelles sur la langue française*, 1660.

28. Cf. Pierre Juliard, *Philosophies of Language in Eighteenth-Century France*, p. 14.

29. Wade, *Studies on Voltaire*, p. 241.

30. Voltaire, *Oeuvres complètes* (ed.) L. Moland, vol. XXX, 2.

31. MS 2376 (*Examen de la Genèse*) and MS 2377 (*Examen des Livres du Nouveau Testament*) in the Bibliothèque de Troyes.

32. I.O. Wade, *Voltaire and Mme du Châtelet* and *The Intellectual Development of Voltaire*.

33. Cf. Wade, *The Intellectual Development of Voltaire*, p. 512.

34. Dom Calmet wrote *Commentaire littéral sur tous les livres de l'Ancien et du Nouveau Testament* as well as an *Histoire généalogique de la maison du Châtelet*.

35. Wade, *The Intellectual Development of Voltaire*, p. 536.

36. R. Mauzi, *L'Idée du bonheur au XVIIIème siècle*, p. 255.

37. J. J. Rousseau, *Discours sur les sciences et les arts*, 1749.

38. Cf. Mauzi, *L'Idée du bonheur au XVIIIème siècle*, p. 437.

Appendix

'Eulogy of Madame la Marquise du Châtelet' by Voltaire*

This translation which France's greatest scholars should have undertaken and which all others need to study is the endeavour and achievement of a lady, to the amazement and the glory of her country. Gabrielle Émilie de Breteuil, wife of the Marquis du Châtelet-Laumont, lieutenant-general of the King's army, is the author of this translation which has become essential to all those desiring to acquire the profound science which the world owes to Newton.

It is much for a woman to know simple geometry, which is not even an introduction to the sublime truths expounded in this immortal work. Clearly, Mme la Marquise du Châtelet must have penetrated deeply into the fields that Newton opened up and mastered the teaching of that great man. We have seen two miracles; one, that Newton wrote this work; the other, that a lady has translated and explained it.

It was not her first labour. She had previously given the public an account of the philosophy of Leibniz, entitled *Institutions de physique adressées à son fils*, a son to whom she had taught geometry herself.

The introductory treatise ('Discours préliminaire') set at the beginning of these *Institutions* is itself a masterpiece of reason and eloquence. And to the other sections of the book she has brought a method and clarity which Leibniz never possessed and which are essential to his ideas, whether one is simply wishing to understand or seeking to refute them.

Once she had rendered the phantasies of Leibniz intelligible — her mind having acquired increasing strength and maturity through this very task — she understood that these metaphysics, so daring yet having so little foundation, were not worthy of her research. Her soul was made for sublime things, but for true ones. She felt that monads and pre-established harmony should be set with Descartes' three elements and that systems which were nothing other than ingenious did not merit her attention. There-

* Translated from 'Éloge historique de Madame la Marquise du Châtelet' (1752) in *Oeuvres complètes*, (ed.) L. Moland, vol. 23, pp. 515–21.

fore, having had the courage to enhance the work of Leibniz, she had the courage to abandon it, a courage that is rare indeed in anyone who has embraced some opinion, but which costs very little effort to a soul impassioned for truth.

Discarding all systematising, she adopted the rule of the Royal Society in London, *nullius in verba*; and because the quality of her mind made her hostile to the spirit of partisanship and to systems, she devoted herself entirely to Newton. At no time did Newton ever have a system which was not based either on the most sublime geometry or on irrefutable experiments. The conjectures he puts forward at the end of his book under the title, 'Enquiries', are only questions; he presents them as nothing else and it would be impossible for one who only ever put forward evident truths not to question everything else.

Everything which is here presented as a principle does indeed deserve that name, namely the basic principles of nature, not known before him; no one can any longer claim to be a scientist without being acquainted with them.

One must therefore be most careful not to look upon this book as presenting a system, that is an assemblage of probables offering either good or bad explanations of certain natural phenomena.

If there were still anyone foolish enough to defend the subtlety of matter or the interaction of matter, to say that the earth is an encrusted sun, that the moon was carried along by the whirl of the earth, that the subtlety of matter causes weight and to uphold all the other phantasies that have been substituted for antiquity's ignorance, one would say: 'That man is a Cartesian'; if he believed in monads, one would say: 'He is a Leibnizian'; but no one will say of one who knows Euclid's 'Elements' that he is a Euclidian; nor of one who knows, since Galileo, the proportion of falling bodies, that he is a Galileist. Similarly, in England, those who have learnt infinitesimal calculus, who have carried out experiments on light, who have learnt about the laws of gravity are not called Newtonians. It is the privilege of errors to lend their name to a sect. If Plato had discovered truths, there would have been no Platonists and all men would little by little have learnt what Plato would have taught; but because, in the ignorance extending throughout the earth, some people held fast to one error, others to a different one, people fought under different banners; there have been peripatetics, Platonists, Epicureans, Xenoists, for want of real philosophers.

If, in France, philosophers who link their knowledge to that with which Newton has endowed the world are still being called Newtonians, this is due to such ignorance and prejudice which still remains. Those who know little and those who do not know properly, and that is a prodigious number, imagine that Newton did nothing but combat Descartes, more or less as he did Gassendi; they have heard of his discoveries and they have taken them to be a new system. In like manner, when Harvey made the circulation of the blood evident, he was opposed in France. Those who dared to adopt the new truth which the public took to be a new opinion, were called Harveyists and circulationists. One has to admit that every discovery has come from abroad and each one has been combated. Even the experiments on light which Newton carried out have been subjected to violent opposition here. After that it is not surprising that when the universal law of gravity of matter had been demonstrated, it was also opposed.

The sublime truths which we owe to Newton were only fully established in France after a whole generation had grown old in the errors of Descartes; for every truth, like every virtue, has the enmity of its contemporaries.

> Turpe putaverunt parere minoribus; et quae
> Imberbes didicere, senes perdende fateri
> (Horace, lib. II, ep. 1,V, 85–6)

Mme du Châtelet has rendered a double service to posterity in translating the book *Principia* and in enriching it with a commentary. True, the Latin tongue in which it is written is understood by all scholars but there is always some fatigue in reading abstract matters in a foreign tongue. Besides, Latin does not have the terms to express truths in those mathematics and physics not possessed by antiquity.

The 'moderns' have had to create new words to render these new ideas. It is a great problem in books about science, and one must admit that it is hardly worthwhile to write such books in a dead language, when one always has to add expressions not known in the ancient world, and this can be awkward. French, a language current throughout Europe, has been enriched by all these new and necessary terms and is much better suited than Latin to spread the new branch of knowledge in the world.

As regards the algebraic commentary, it is a work above that of a translation. Mme du Châtelet has based her work here on the ideas of M. Clairaut. She worked out the calculations and when she had completed a chapter, M. Clairaut checked and corrected it. That is not all; in such a painstaking work a mistake can slip in: it is very easy, when writing, to substitute one sign for another. M. Clairaut has had the calculations checked by a third person, once they were written out; so that it is morally impossible that a mistake due to an oversight should have slipped into this work; equally that a work in which M. Clairaut has had a hand, could be other than excellent of its kind.

The more astonishing it is that a woman should have been capable of an enterprise that required such penetration and so persistent a labour, the more must her premature death be deplored. She had not finished the commentary entirely when she foresaw that death would carry her off. She was jealous for her reputation and had none of the pride of false modesty which seems to despise something one desires and seems to be above true fame — the only reward of those who serve the public, the only one worthy of great souls, one which it is good to seek and which only those incapable of attaining it affect to hold in contempt. It was this concern for her reputation which made her determined, a few days before she died, to deposit her book, entirely written in her hand, in the King's Library.

To this appreciation of fame, she added a simplicity that does not always accompany it but which is often a feature of serious study. No woman was ever more *savante*, 'learned', than she was, yet no one deserved less than she did to be called *femme savante* [blue-stocking]. She only ever spoke about science to those from whom she thought she could learn; never did she discuss it to attract attention to herself. She was not ever seen gathering around her those circles which wage battles of the mind, where one sets up a kind of tribunal and passes judgement on one's century — which then, in its turn, it judges you most severely. For a long time she moved in circles which did not know her worth and she paid no attention to such ignorance.

The ladies, playing cards with her in the company of the queen, were far from suspecting that they were sitting next to Newton's commentator. She was taken for an ordinary person; only occasionally were people amazed at the speed and accuracy with which she would reckon and complete differentials; as soon as something needed to be worked out, the *philosophe* in her could not remain hidden. I saw her, one day, divide a nine-figure number by nine other figures, in her head, without any help, in the presence of a geometer unable to keep up with her.

Born with singular eloquence, that eloquence was not used by her unless the subject merited it: those writings which only seek to display wit; the subtleties, the delicate turns of phrase in which one couches ordinary ideas, did not enter her immense talents. Apt terms, precision, accuracy and forcefulness characterise her style. Her writing is closer to that of Pascal and Nicole than to that of Mme de Sévigné. Yet the firm discipline and the vigorous character of her mind did not render her inaccessible to the beauty of sentiment. She was affected by the charm of poetry and of eloquence and no ear was ever more sensitive to harmony. She knew the best poetry by heart and could not suffer mediocre verse. She had this advantage over Newton that she combined the deep thinking of philosophy with the keenest and most delicate taste for letters. One can only feel pity for any philosopher reduced to arid truths, one for whom the beauty of imagination and sentiment are lost.

From her tenderest youth, her mind was nourished by reading good authors in more than one language. She had begun a translation of the *Aeneid* and I have seen several sections of this imbued with the soul of the author. Later she learnt Italian and English; Tasso and Milton were as familiar to her as Virgil; she made less progress in Spanish because she was told that in this language there was only one famous book and that that book was frivolous.

The study of her own language was one of her chief occupations. There are remarks by her still in manuscript where, in the midst of the uncertainties and oddities of grammar, one sees that *philosophe* spirit which should prevail everywhere and which provides the guiding thread in every labyrinth.

In the midst of so much work which even the most industrious scholar might hardly have taken upon himself, who will believe that she found the time not only to fulfil all of her obligations in society, but eagerly to seek its every entertainment. She was equally devoted to the best in society and to study. All things that matter to society concerned her, except slander. She was never heard to point to a single foolishness. She had neither the time nor the inclination to take notice of such things and when told that certain persons had not done her justice, she would reply that she did not wish to know. She was, one day, shown some pitiful pamphlet or other, the author of which, having had no means of knowing about her, had dared speak ill of her. She said that the author had wasted time writing about these pointless matters and that she did not intend to waste hers reading them; the next day, learning that the author of the libellous pamphlet had been put in prison, she wrote to plead in his favour, without his ever finding out.

She was missed at the court of France as much as one can be in a land where personal interest makes one so easily forget all else. Her memory is treasured by all who knew her intimately and who were capable of perceiving the breadth of her mind and the greatness of her soul.

It would have been better for her friends had she not undertaken this work from which scholars will benefit; in mourning her fate, one might well say: *periit . . . arte sua* (Ovid, Ibis, 6).

She believed that death was striking long before the blow fell that has taken her from us. From that time on, her one thought was to make use of the little time she foresaw as still left to her to complete what she had undertaken and to deprive death of what she regarded as the best part of herself. Ardent and persevering work, the continual lack of sleep at a time when rest might have saved her, finally brought about the death she had foreseen. She felt the end approaching and with singularly mixed feelings which seemed to struggle with one another, she apparently regretted leaving life and yet looked boldly on death. The sorrow of eternal separation visibly afflicted her soul and yet the philosophy which filled that soul enabled all her courage to stay with her. The image of a man sadly tearing himself away from his distressed family and calmly making preparations for a long journey would in a faint way depict her sorrow and her firmness; so that those who witnessed her last moments felt her loss doubly through their distress and her regrets while admiring the strength of her spirit, which mingled such touching regret to such unshaken constancy.

Mme du Châtelet died at the palace of Lunéville, on 10 September 1749, at the age of forty-three years and six months and was buried in the neighbouring chapel.

Chronology

Date	Mme du Châtelet	Cultural events	Historical events
1706	Birth of Gabrielle-Emilie de Breteuil		
1710		Leibniz, *Essai de Théodicée sur la bonté de Dieu, la liberté de l'homme et l'origine du mal*	
1711		Steele and Addison found the *Spectator*	
1713		Archaeological find at Herculaneum	Papal Bull *Ugenitus* against Jansenism
1715			Death of Louis XIV
1716		Death of Leibniz	
1717			Peter the Great of Russia visits Paris
1718			Death of Charles XII of Sweden
1721		Montesquieu, *Les Lettres persanes* Death of Watteau	
1723			Death of the French Regent
1725	Marriage to Florent-Claude Chastellet		Marriage of Louis XV of France to Maria Leczszinski
1726	Birth of a daughter	Swift, *Gulliver's Travels*	Cardinal Fleury becomes Minister of State
1727	Birth of a son	Death of Newton	
1728	Death of Mme du Châtelet's father	Voltaire, *La Henriade*	

1730		Voltaire, *Brutus* Marivaux, *Le Jeu de l'amour et du hasard*	Robert Walpole becomes Prime Minister in England
1731		Voltaire, *Histoire de Charles XII* Prévost, *Manon Lescaut*	
1732		Voltaire, *Zaïre, Histoire de Charles XII*	
1733	Beginning of friendship with Voltaire	Voltaire, *Lettres anglaises* published in England	
1734	Mme du Châtelet and Voltaire go to live in Cirey	*Lettres anglaises ou Lettres philosophiques* condemned	Abdication of King Stanislas Leczszinski, father of the Queen of France
1735	Begins translation of Mandeville's *Fable of the Bees*	Rameau, *Indes galantes*, opera–ballet Voltaire–Desfontaines quarrel	
1736	Works on *Grammaire raisonnée*	Voltaire, *Le Mondain*	
1737	Submits essay 'Sur la Nature du feu' to Académie des Sciences; works on *Examen de la Genèse* (1737–42)	Voltaire, *Eléments de la philosophie de Newton*; works on *Traité de métaphysique* (1734–8).	
1738		Samuel Johnson, *London*. Scientific expedition led by Maupertuis returns. Voltaire–Desfontaines quarrel	The Duchy of Lorraine given to Stanislas Leczszinska,
1739	Law suit in Belgium; Mme du Châtelet and Voltaire go there Dispute with Mairan		Marriage of Louise Elisabeth de Bourbon to son of Philip of

	on dynamic force in matter	Spain
1740	*Institutions de physique*	Crown Prince Frederick of Prussia becomes King Frederick II
1742		Voltaire, *Mahomet*	
1743		Voltaire, *Mérope*	Death of Cardinal Fleury
1745		Voltaire, *Le Poème de Fontenoy*	French victory at Fontenoy
1746	Works on *Discours sur le Bonheur* (1746–8)	Diderot, *Pensées philosophiques* Condillac, *Essai sur l'origine des connaissances humaines*	Death of Philip V of Spain. French take Brussels
1747		Voltaire, *Zadig*	
1748	Mme du Châtelet and Voltaire are guests of Stanislas Leczszinski at Lunéville	Richardson, *Clarrisa Harlowe* Montesquieu, *L'Esprit de lois* Archaeological find at Pompeii	End of Austrian War of Succession
1749	Second visit to Lunéville. Completes translation and commentary on Newton's *Principia mathematica*. Dies at Lunéville on 10 September		

Select Bibliography

Works by Mme du Châtelet

Lettres de la Marquise du Châtelet, introduction and notes by T. Besterman, 2 vols, Geneva, Institutions et Musée Voltaire, 1958.

Lettres inédites de Madame la Marquise du Châtelet à Monsieur le Comte d'Argental auxquelles on a joint une dissertation sur l'existence de Dieu, les réflexions sur le bonheur par le même auteur et deux notices historiques sur Mme du Châtelet et M. d'Argental, Paris, 1806.

Examen de la Genèse and *Examen des Livres du Nouveau Testament*, MSS. 2376 and 2377 in Bibliothèque de Troyes (MSS. are not signed).

'Lettre sur les "Eléments de la philosophie de Newton" ', in *Journal des savants*, September 1738.

Institutions de physique, Paris, Prault, 1740.

Réponse de Mme xxx à la lettre de M. de Mairan sur la question des forces vives, Brussels, Foppens, 1741.

Dissertation sur la nature et la propagation du feu, Paris, Prault, 1744.

Discours sur le bonheur, introduction and commentary by Robert Mauzi, Paris, 1961.

The Fable of the Bees, by Mandeville, transl.; *Essai sur l'optique* (one chapter); *Grammaire raisonnée* (three chapters), in Ira O. Wade, *Studies on Voltaire with some unpublished papers of Mme du Châtelet*, Princeton, NJ, Princeton University Press, 1947.

Principes mathématiques de la philosophie naturelle, par M. Newton, traduits par feue Madame la Marquise du Châtelet, Paris, 1759.

Works on Madame du Châtelet

Badinter, E., *Emilie, Emilie: l'ambition féminine au XVIII⁰ siècle*, Paris, Flammarion, 1983.

Créqui, Marquise de, *Souvenirs de la Marquise de Créqui*, (ed.) Maurice Cousin, 3 vols., Paris, 1834–5.

Edwards, S., *The Divine Mistress*, London, Cassell, 1971.

Deffand, Mme du, *Correspondance complète*, (ed.) Lescure, Paris, Plon, 1865.

Formey, J.-H., *Souvenirs d'un citoyen*, Berlin, 1789.

Graffigny, Mme de F.-P., *Vie privée de Voltaire et de Mme du Châtelet*, Paris, 1820.

Hamel, F., *An Eighteenth-Century Marquise: A Study of Émilie du Châtelet and her Times*, London, 1910.

Longchamp, *Voltaire et Mme du Châtelet*, Paris, 1863.

Maurel, A., *La Marquise du Châtelet, amie de Voltaire*, Paris, Hachette, 1930.

Mitford, N., *Voltaire in Love*, London, Hamish Hamilton, 1957.

Vaillot, R., *Madame du Châtelet*, Paris, Albin Michel, 1978. (This is, in fact, the authoritative biography.)

General Works and Studies Cited

D'Alembert, 'Essai des elements de philosophie', in *Oeuvres philosophiques historiques et littéraires*, Paris, 1805.

Algarotti, F., *Il Newtonianismo per le dame*, Naples, 1737.

d'Allemagne, H.R., *Les Cartes à jouer du 14ème au 20ème siècle*, Paris, 1906.

Barber, W.H., *Leibniz in France*, Oxford, Clarendon Press, 1955.

Biographie universelle par une Société de Gens de Lettres, Paris, Michaud, 1844.

Calmet, Dom A., *Commentaire littéral sur tous les livres de l'ancien et du nouveau Testament*, 23 vols., Paris, 1707–16.

———, *Histoire généalogique de la maison du Châtelet*, Nancy, 1741.

Cohen, I.B., 'The French Translation of Isaac Newton's *Philosophiae Naturalis Principia Mathematica*', in *Archives Internationales d'histoire des sciences*, nos 84–5, Paris, 1968.

Correspondance littéraire, philosophique et critique, par Grimm, Diderot, Raynal, Meister, et al., 16 vols, Paris, Garnier Frères, 1877–82.

Cotton, C., *The Compleat Gamester*, London, 1725.

Diderot, *Oeuvres philosophiques*, Paris, Garnier Frères, 1964.

G. Doscot, *Stanislas Leczszinski et la cour de Lorraine*, Lausanne, Editions Rencontre, 1969.

J. Dunkley, *Gambling, a Social and Moral Problem in France, 1685–1792*, Studies on Voltaire and the Eighteenth Century, vol. 235, Oxford, The Voltaire Foundation, 1985.

Encyclopédie ou dictionnaire raisonné des sciences, des arts et des métiers, par une Sociéte de Gens de Lettres, mis en ordre et publié par M. Diderot, 17 vols. plus plates, Paris, Le Breton, 1751–65.

Fontenelle, *Entretiens sur la pluralité des mondes, Oeuvres,* Paris, 1742.

L. Gardiner Janik, 'Searching for the metaphysics of science: the structure and composition of Mme du Châtelet's *Institutions de physique,* 1737–40', in *Studies on Voltaire and the Eighteenth Century,* (ed.) T. Besterman, vol. 201, Geneva, Institutions et Musée Voltaire, 1982.

Grammaire générale et raisonnée contenant les fondements de l'art de parler expliqués d'une manière claire et naturelle, les raisons de ce qui est commun à toutes les langues et des principales différences qui s'y rencontrent, et plusieurs remarques nouvelles sur la langue française, Paris, 1660.

Juliard, P., *Philosophies of Language in Eighteenth-Century France,* The Hague, Mouton, 1970.

Launay, M., and Mailhos, G., *Introduction à la vie littéraire du XVIIIème siècle,* Paris, Bordas, 1984.

J. Lough, *An Introduction to Eighteenth-Century France,* London, Longman, 1960.

Mandeville, B., *The Fable of the Bees,* (ed.) P. Harth, Harmondsworth, Penguin, 1970.

Mauzi, R., *L'Idée du bonheur au XVIIIème siècle,* Paris, Armand Colin, 1969.

Niklaus, R., 'The Age of Enlightenment', in *The Age of Enlightenment, Studies presented to T. Besterman,* University of St Andrews, 1967.

Pellison, M., *Les Hommes de lettres au 18ème siècle,* Paris, 1911.

Roger, J., *Les Sciences de la vie dans la pensée française au XVIIIème siècle,* Paris, Armand Colin, 1971.

Rousseau, J.-J., *Oeuvres complètes,* 13 vols., Paris, Hachette, 1865–70.

Toussaint, *Des Moeurs,* Paris, 1748.

Voltaire, *Oeuvres complètes,* (ed.) L. Moland, 1879.

Ira O. Wade, *Voltaire and Mme du Châtelet: An Essay on the Intellectual Activity at Cirey,* Princeton, NJ, Princeton University Press, 1941.

———, *The Intellectual Development of Voltaire,* Princeton, NJ, Princeton University Press, 1969.

Index